Cambridge English Readers

Level 6

Series editor: Philip Prowse

A Dangerous Sky

Michael Austen

CAMBRIDGE
UNIVERSITY PRESS

CAMBRIDGE
UNIVERSITY PRESS

University Printing House, Cambridge CB2 8BS, United Kingdom

One Liberty Plaza, 20th Floor, New York, NY 10006, USA

477 Williamstown Road, Port Melbourne, VIC 3207, Australia

314–321, 3rd Floor, Plot 3, Splendor Forum, Jasola District Centre, New Delhi – 110025, India

79 Anson Road, #06–04/06, Singapore 079906

Cambridge University Press is part of the University of Cambridge.

It furthers the University's mission by disseminating knowledge in the pursuit of education, learning and research at the highest international levels of excellence.

www.cambridge.org
Information on this title: www.cambridge.org/9781107694057

First published 2013

Michael Austen has asserted his right to be identified as the Author of the Work in accordance with the Copyright, Designs and Patents Act 1988.

Printed in Great Britain by Ashford Colour Press Ltd.

Typeset by Aptara Inc.
Map artwork by Malcolm Barnes
Illustration by Bob Moulder

A catalogue record of this book is available from the British Library.

ISBN 978-1-107-694057 paperback

Contents

Characters

Francesca Bartolli: an eighteen-year-old au pair
Doug Barker: a flying instructor at Fastwings
Mrs Thompson: Francesca's employer
Sam and Emma: Mrs Thompson's children
Tom Brennan: the office manager at Flying Start
George Scott: a flying instructor at Flying Start

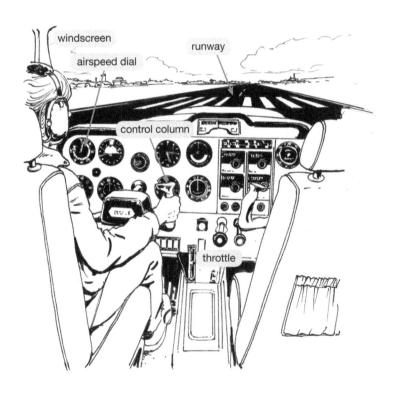

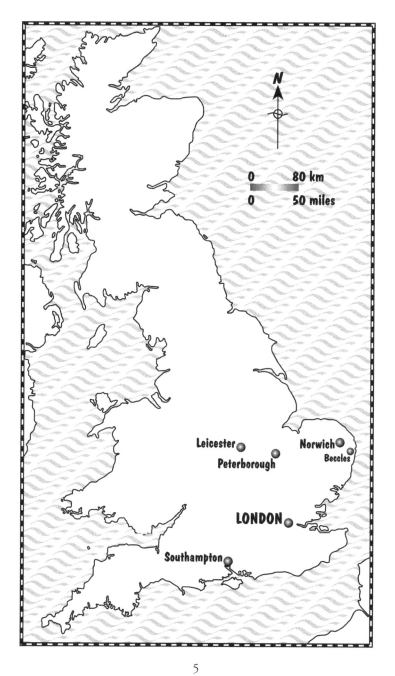

N

0   80 km
0   50 miles

Leicester
Peterborough
Norwich
Beccles

LONDON

Southampton

Chapter 1   *Control!*

'Golf Bravo Alpha. You are cleared for take-off.'

Eighteen-year-old Swiss-Italian, Francesca Bartolli, sat in the small single-engined Cessna 152 and stared through the window at the runway ahead. A white dotted line stretched down the middle of the concrete far into the distance. Had the moment finally arrived? Was she really going to pilot a plane at last?

'Well?' said a voice in her headphones. 'What are you waiting for?' It was Doug, the flying instructor, in the seat beside her.

Francesca felt hot. The sun was shining brightly through the windscreen, turning the plane's small cockpit into an oven. And the headphones were tight and painful on her ears. 'You mean you want me to …' she began.

'Push the throttle in smoothly and hold the control column steady,' the instructor said. 'When I tell you, just pull back gently. I'll do all the rest.'

'OK,' Francesca answered in a shaky voice.

Doug called the control tower for permission to take off, but Francesca didn't take in what he said. Now that the moment had finally arrived, she suddenly wondered if it was really what she wanted.

The instructor's voice became firmer. 'Right, let's go!' he said.

Francesca didn't hesitate now. Setting her mouth with new determination, she stretched out her right arm and pushed carefully on the throttle. Immediately, the engine roared and the little aircraft seemed to sit up. The next moment it was being pulled forward as if on a huge elastic band. Within a couple of seconds, they were already racing along the runway. The white dotted lines began disappearing quickly below the nose of the plane.

'Keep your eye on the airspeed dial,' she heard the instructor say in her headphones again, above the roar of the engine. 'When the needle reaches 60, pull back gently.'

Francesca didn't answer. There was so much to look at, so much going on. It seemed somehow crazy, this race down the runway. She watched the needle going round the dial: 40 ... 45 ... The white dotted lines on the runway flashed below the plane. Her head felt as if it was bursting. All of a sudden, the needle was at 60.

'Right, pull back!' came Doug's voice.

But already Francesca was pulling back on the control column. It was much lighter than she expected, just like pulling your hand slowly through cream. Straightaway the nose of the aircraft lifted and the runway disappeared from view. The next moment she felt the plane rise into the air.

'OK, hold it there!' said Doug.

Francesca felt a strange smile pull at the sides of her mouth. She couldn't help it. They were flying!

'That's enough! Keep the nose down. Don't climb too fast. Keep your eye on that airspeed dial. Climb at 80. 80's the perfect climb.'

Francesca wanted to look around. Already the airfield was beginning to slip away below, and new fields were coming into view, but Francesca had to keep her eye on the airspeed dial. The needle was dropping. 70 ... 65 ...

'Nose down! Keep it down!'

Francesca pushed the control column forward quickly. The engine roared and the plane began bouncing up and down. She pulled back, trying to correct the movement, but then the wings began rolling. She felt a bit desperate; everything was going wrong.

'OK,' said Doug, 'I have control.' He reached out to the control column in front of him and the plane began flying steadily. Francesca felt her face burn red with shame.

'I'm sorry,' she said. 'I didn't mean …' She couldn't even finish.

'Don't worry about it,' Doug answered. 'Everyone finds it difficult at first.'

She glanced across at the man. He was smiling at her.

'Just relax,' he said. 'I'll take us up a bit higher, then we can level out and you can try again.'

Francesca watched as the instructor settled the plane into a proper climb, then looked out through the side window. A sick feeling was rising up inside her. Was flying really going to be so much harder than she'd imagined? She'd been looking forward to this moment for so long, dreamed of piloting a plane for so many years – surely it wasn't going to be a disappointment after all?

'You OK?' Doug called. Francesca didn't look round. She was determined not to let the man see her nerves.

'Yes, fine,' she answered. She looked down. She saw a farm pass beneath them; the buildings getting smaller even as she looked. Then there was a road. Already the cars on it looked like toys that she might reach out and pick up in her hand. Next a wood slid below, and the silvery S-shape of a river, then the sharp brown line of a railway.

At last, when Francesca felt in control of herself again, she began looking round the cockpit. She stared at all the dials and switches in front of her. Would they ever make sense to her? She must have shaken her head slightly.

'Confusing?' the instructor's voice came.

She could see him smiling again.

'Yes,' she answered. 'Yes, they are.'

'You'll get used to them. Just remember where the airspeed dial is – that's the most important. Speed through the air. That's what keeps you flying.'

Francesca nodded and looked for the airspeed dial again. There it was in the top left-hand corner, the needle pointing directly to 80.

The instructor made another quick call to the control tower, so sudden and rapid that Francesca didn't catch it. Then he glanced across at her once more.

'So, how long have you been in England?' he asked.

'Six months,' Francesca answered.

The man nodded. 'They did a good job at the language centre,' he said. 'Your English is very impressive.'

'Thank you,' Francesca answered. 'I did ten years of English at school, so it wasn't starting from zero.'

'And you didn't fancy university?' the instructor asked. 'Came straight here to England when you left school?'

'Yes,' Francesca replied. 'My parents tried to make me do a degree, but all I've ever wanted is to learn to fly and become a commercial pilot. In the end, my father said, "Well, if I don't have to pay for university, I suppose I can pay for a language school and some flying lessons." And as English is the language of aviation, England's the best place to learn to fly.'

Doug replied with a nod. 'So, what will you do after this? You realise the commercial pilot's course is ten times the cost of the private pilot's licence you're doing with me?'

'Yes, I know,' Francesca answered. 'But I'm working as an au pair for the family I live with here. And then when I go back to Switzerland I'll get a job and give extra English classes in the evening. I'm hoping I can make plenty of money like that.'

Francesca saw Doug glance across at her. For a moment a smile played around his lips again as if an idea had occurred to him, but then he said very simply, 'You are a very determined young lady, Francesca.'

Francesca looked back into the man's dark sunglasses, but couldn't see his eyes. 'I am,' she said quietly. 'Yes, I am.'

Doug turned his attention back to the controls. Francesca watched him push the control column forward very slowly. As the nose of the plane dropped, suddenly the horizon came into view through the windscreen. Francesca felt their speed increasing rapidly, and when she looked at the airspeed dial, she saw it was already pointing to 120. A few moments later, Doug reached for the throttle and the speed dropped back a little.

'Right,' he said. 'We're flying straight and level now. You take control again and see if you can keep the plane steady like this.'

Very firmly, Francesca took hold of the controls once more. For two or three seconds as she took over, the plane started bouncing around again.

'Gently!' Doug called. 'You don't need to hold the controls so tightly. Imagine you're with your boyfriend,' he added with a little laugh.

Francesca gave a small frown, but concentrated on the control column. She relaxed her grip slightly. The plane seemed to respond. Slowly, she moved the control column around with tiny actions. It was strange. The plane seemed to fly itself somehow, as if it were an animal, a horse perhaps, which was just beginning to trust its rider.

'That's better!' Doug called. 'That's the idea.'

Francesca felt her confidence returning. Gradually, she increased the movements she made, watching and feeling how the plane responded. Slowly, a strange feeling came over her. She felt as though she wasn't sitting in the cockpit holding the control column, but instead had her arms stretched out, like a child pretending to have wings. And as she imagined this – seeing herself as the pilot of her dreams – the wings of the plane seemed to melt into her own. It felt like a miracle. She was flying all alone.

All of a sudden she glanced across the cockpit. Doug was staring at her, and nodding his head very slowly.

'Very good,' he said. 'I'm full of admiration.'

Chapter 2   *The price of dreams*

Two hours later, Francesca was on the bus home, heading back to Norwich. As the bus wound its way slowly through the streets, Francesca looked out of the window at the dull buildings and relived her first flight. It was hard to believe that she'd really been piloting a plane up in the sky only a short time before. It felt almost like a dream. But she had, and the lesson had gone well. No, that wasn't true, she told herself – the lesson had gone brilliantly, and she hadn't just made that up herself. The instructor had said so. He had told her she was a 'natural'. Francesca felt wonderfully happy.

She thought back over the day and her arrival at the airfield. She'd imagined Fastwings to be a busy little flying school with several other students, but when she'd arrived and discovered hers was the only lesson that day, it had made her feel uncomfortable. So had Doug's welcome when she'd walked through the Fastwings office door. 'Well, this is a pleasant surprise,' he'd said. 'These lessons might be rather more fun than I'd imagined.'

Francesca tried to decide what she thought of Doug. She felt confused. He was about thirty-five or forty, quite tall and good-looking. However, that first remark of his was just the sort of thing she'd hoped she wouldn't hear in England. And there was something in his eyes she didn't like. But then that had passed, and she had the flying lesson to concentrate on. There was no doubt he was a very good pilot and he'd made her feel good about her flying. It was just the way he looked at her and his odd remarks that made her feel uncomfortable. She was used to such comments from Italian men, who were always trying to show off in front of women. But Doug was English and she thought Englishmen might be different. What had he said about handling the control column like her boyfriend? Did it mean what she thought?

Francesca felt her heart drop all of a sudden as the image of Andrea came crashing back into her head. Dear Andrea. The break up of their relationship was almost too painful a memory: the last three months in Ticino, before she came over to England, had been so emotional. Andrea had been her first – well, her only real boyfriend. They'd begun going out together when Francesca was only fifteen. And she'd loved him deeply. Dear Andrea, funny, handsome, sexy Andrea – the boy she'd given herself to – the boy she'd imagined marrying and having children with.

But Andrea hadn't wanted her to come to Britain. He hadn't wanted Francesca to learn to fly. He'd always said her plan to become an airline pilot was ridiculous, an embarrassment to him, something he couldn't possibly ever accept. And he'd meant it. Whenever Francesca had raised the subject, he'd become angry, once even marching out of a café in front of all her friends with a cry of 'Stupid, selfish dreamer!' Well, who was the selfish one? What kind of love was it that wanted to cut your wings? And what was wrong with having a dream?

In the end, Francesca had decided their relationship would never work. But making that decision, and finishing things with Andrea, had almost broken her heart. She'd made up her mind then that nothing, and no one, would ever stand in the way of her flying dream. She wasn't interested in a relationship with anyone.

The sight of a familiar pub brought Francesca back to the present. The next bus stop was hers. She hurried off the bus and turned in the direction of home. She had a job as an au pair with the Thompson family, looking after the two children, Sam and Emma. That afternoon Mrs Thompson was picking the children up from school, so Francesca only had to prepare their dinner, and get them ready for bed. After that, she was free – well, free only to continue studying all the instruction books necessary for the pilot's licence exams: aviation law, radio procedures, the weather, all the technical matters … the amount was terrifying.

A pretty scarf in a shop window caught her eye. She hesitated. To her surprise, it wasn't very expensive: only £11.99. Not very much to spend, she said to herself.

A moment later she dragged herself away from the shop window. She couldn't afford it. If she wanted to achieve her ambition, there could be no luxuries. She had to save and save and save! Everything now was a question of money. Flying was so hugely expensive! Lessons were more than £140 an hour and the minimum required for the private pilot's licence was forty-five hours. She'd arranged with Doug to have two one-hour lessons a week over the following six months, on Tuesday and Thursday afternoons – the days Mrs Thompson only worked in the mornings. But, in order to get a discount, she'd paid Doug in advance for the whole course, including examinations, and equipment – and the total was over £7000! And if she needed more than forty-five hours for the private pilot's licence, she would have to pay extra. Even though her father had agreed to pay £5000 now and then help fund the commercial pilot training, the amounts required were frightening. As an au pair, although her room and food were paid for, she only received £50 a week – less than half-an-hour's flying lesson.

Mrs Thompson was waiting for her when she got home. 'So, how was it?' she asked.

Francesca couldn't help grinning. 'Fantastic!' she said. 'I'm so excited. The instructor said I was very good.'

'Wonderful,' Mrs Thompson replied. 'But now you need to call your mother. She telephoned ten minutes ago, terrified that you might have had an accident.'

Francesca shook her head in despair. Her mother's fears were yet another stress she had to handle.

Francesca went upstairs, opened up her laptop to make a Skype call, then listened to the familiar sound as the number rang in Ticino. After only a couple of seconds, her mother's anxious face appeared on the screen. A rush of Italian followed.

'Francesca! Francesca, my darling, is that you? Are you all right? Why didn't you phone? Your father and I have been worried sick!' said her mother.

'Mamma!' Francesca said, when she finally managed to get in a word. 'Calm down! I've only just got home. Everything's fine.'

'Oh, thank God for that!' her mother replied. 'I haven't been able to do anything all day, imagining you crashing the stupid plane. Please say you didn't enjoy it and that you've decided to come home.'

Francesca closed her eyes. After a couple of seconds she took a deep breath. 'No, Mamma,' she said. 'It was brilliant. Mamma, you must try not to worry. The instructor called me "a natural". It was even better than I'd dreamed!'

Chapter 3   *A different kind of fun*

'Right,' Doug said, looking across the cockpit at Francesca, 'I think it's about time we had a bit of fun.'

'What do you mean?' Francesca answered.

'Well, there are all kinds of fun,' Doug replied with a strange smile. 'But the fun I'm referring to is stalling.'

Francesca felt confused. 'I'm sorry, I don't understand,' she said. She wasn't certain whether he was making a joke, but in any case the word 'stalling' was a new one for her.

'A stall,' Doug replied, becoming more serious, 'is when the plane stops flying – usually when it isn't going fast enough for the wings to do their job. In other words, when a plane is in danger of falling out of the sky!'

It was a fortnight later – two weeks after Francesca's first lesson. She'd had three more lessons since and things couldn't be going better. In the second lesson she'd had further practice at flying straight and level. Then she'd gone on to 'turns': 'banking' the plane – rolling the plane to the left and right; and also 'the climb', which seemed so difficult in her first lesson. Doug kept telling her how pleased he was with her. He had even said if she continued at the same rate of progress, he could imagine her taking her first solo flight in a couple of weeks' time – after perhaps only ten hours – much faster than the average student.

But now Francesca felt a tiny stab of fear. Doug still had this slightly cruel look on his face. She was beginning to think he quite enjoyed it when she was frightened.

Francesca tried to focus on the lesson again. 'So, what are we going to do then?' she asked as lightly as she could.

'Well,' Doug replied, 'we're going to fly the plane up to 4000 feet, check there's no one else about, and then you're going to cut the power until the plane stops flying.' Doug paused, the sunglasses he always wore flashing in the sunlight.

'What happens then?' Francesca asked, trying to disguise the slight tremble in her voice.

'Well, then, I hope you're going to get the plane flying again.' Doug paused and smiled. 'Otherwise we'll make a horrible mess in a field!'

Fifteen minutes later, they took off and began climbing into the grey sky. It was a dull day, not the bright clear weather that Francesca had experienced for her other lessons. When they reached 4000 feet Francesca set the plane up for straight and level flight, but it was much more difficult than in her last lessons. The grey of the land and the grey of the sky meant there was almost no horizon – no guide for keeping level. She started to feel nervous.

They flew on for five minutes until they were out over farmland to the west of the city. Then, after glancing around out of the cockpit window, Doug spoke again.

'Right,' he said. 'First, check your safety harness.'

Francesca pulled against the harness, but she was held so tight against the seat she could barely move.

'Good,' Doug went on, once he'd checked his own harness. 'Right, now we look around: to the right … and the left … now a quick look behind … and most important of all, down below … Anything about?'

Francesca searched the sky, but couldn't see any other aircraft. 'No,' she answered.

'OK, now listen carefully,' Doug continued. 'In a moment you're going to pull out the throttle so there's no power, and pull back on the control column to keep the nose up in the air. At some point you'll feel the plane tremble and the controls will go soft like jelly. And the stall-warning alarm behind us will sound – it's like a trumpet sound. Then, all of a sudden the nose will drop. When that happens, push the control column forward – this is very important. Don't pull it back, which seems the natural thing to do – push forward so that you're heading towards the ground. If you don't do that, the plane won't start flying again. After a few seconds like that, the plane will pick up flying speed and you can pull out of the dive and add the power again.'

He looked across at Francesca. 'OK, do you understand?'

Francesca repeated the instructions back. Her heart was beating a little faster, unsure of exactly what lay ahead.

'Ready?' Doug asked.

Francesca nodded.

'Right,' he said. 'Now, pull out the throttle.'

Francesca obeyed. Almost immediately the power died away and the nose began to drop.

'Pull back!' Doug called.

Francesca did as he said. The control column was firm, much firmer than she'd felt before.

'Harder!' Doug shouted. 'Pull back! Keep the nose up!'

It required all Francesca's strength to keep pulling back. She felt herself becoming more and more anxious. It was partly because of the way the plane was behaving, but partly Doug's shouting as well. Her heart was racing.

'Keep pulling back!' he called. 'Harder! Come on!'

Suddenly the stall-warning alarm sounded – a long steady noise that didn't stop. For a moment the plane trembled, then all at once, the wings seemed to fold.

For the next couple of seconds Francesca didn't know what was happening. Her stomach seemed to fall out of her body. Suddenly she found she was staring at the ground and the earth was racing up to meet them. A scream became trapped in her throat; she was paralysed with fear. The thought rushed through her head that she was going to die, that this was it, that the flying idea had been a terrible mistake. She didn't know what to do.

The next moment she realised Doug had taken over the controls. Still with the scream caught in her throat, she saw him take his control column firmly in both hands and push forward, increasing the angle of their dive, then slowly pull back. After a few seconds he had brought back the power and they were flying straight and level again.

For a short while Francesca felt nothing but relief. Then she felt her face burning with shame.

Doug was watching her closely. 'You OK?'

'F…fine,' Francesca stammered. She felt angry all of a sudden. 'I … it just took me by surprise, that's all,' she said.

Doug smiled. 'Yes,' he replied quietly. 'It's a bit of a shock the first time. Just a matter of letting yourself go,' he added lightly. 'Like some other kind of fun I can think of. In time you might actually get to like it.'

As he said so, he looked across again and rested a hand on Francesca's knee. For a moment she didn't realise what had happened. Then she threw him a look of astonishment. A couple of seconds later he withdrew his hand. They flew on in silence and neither referred to what had happened.

Chapter 4 *Have no fear!*

That night Francesca couldn't sleep, her mind was so full of unpleasant thoughts. The incident that afternoon had reminded her of the manager of a café where she'd worked for the summer a couple of years before. With a feeling of sickness, she remembered the horrible man purposely pushing past her as she worked behind the counter, pressing himself against her and pretending it was an accident. Although it had happened four or five times, she'd done nothing and said nothing, instead deciding the best thing was simply to change jobs. But the incident had both embarrassed and angered her. Now the memory of Doug's words and his hand on her knee gave her the same miserable feeling. Had she misunderstood what he was saying? Had his hand simply been a friendly gesture to reassure her? Or was it something else? Was he trying to suggest something to her?

After half an hour like this, she finally sat up, switched on the bedside light, and decided to think logically about what had happened. Taking her iPod from the drawer, she put on the headphones, selected some gentle music, and slowly felt herself calm down. Then she thought back to that afternoon's incident.

Had it really happened? Yes, of course, it had. Was it an accident? No, of course, it wasn't. But that didn't necessarily mean Doug had a sexual motive. Stalling the aircraft had seriously alarmed her and he might have been genuinely trying to reassure her. But was it acceptable for a man to put his hand on her knee like that? She wished desperately there was another woman taking lessons for her to talk to, but there wasn't. There seemed to be only two other students, in fact – both men, and she had yet to see either of them. When Francesca had asked where the other students were, Doug had simply said, 'Well, times are hard, didn't you know?' And then, 'Why? What's the problem?'

Francesca tried to think what she knew about Doug already. She was sure he was married. Once when she was waiting in the office, Doug had taken a phone call, discussing the time he'd be home that evening. Francesca remembered that as he'd put down the phone he'd made one of those typically British comments she couldn't be certain was a joke – something about 'the joys of marriage'. She guessed, too, that he had children: a picture frame on his desk contained a photo of two pretty young girls – twins of six or seven, she thought. But did it make any difference whether he was married with children? Her experience at the café had taught her that it didn't. That dirty old man had a wife and three horrible teenage boys, who used to sit around the café, grinning at her in almost as disgusting a manner as the old man's.

For a moment or two she considered searching for Doug Barker on the Internet and seeing what she could discover about him, then decided it was ridiculous. She switched off her iPod, turned out the light and determined to get some rest. It was half an hour more before sleep finally came.

* * *

By the time of her next lesson, two days later, the whole 'hand-on-the-knee' business seemed like a crazy dream and her spirits lifted again. Flying was the important thing. She had to concentrate on that.

She was a little late when she arrived at the airfield that afternoon. Doug was in the hangar where the planes were kept, checking the Cessna's engine.

'So, you've come after all,' he said, without looking round. 'I was afraid the last lesson might have frightened you off.'

Francesca hesitated for a moment, wondering exactly what he meant, then she answered, 'Not at all. My bus was held up in the traffic, that's all.'

Doug turned to look at her and smiled. 'Good,' he said. 'It would be a terrible shame after such a promising beginning.'

To Francesca's relief, Doug seemed to be in a very business-like mood that day. They dragged the plane outside and began by checking round the aircraft. Although she'd helped with the checks in her previous lessons, Doug hadn't spent very long explaining all the procedures. This time he did. Francesca was impressed at how careful it all was: walking round the plane, examining all the moving parts, looking at the tyres, pushing and pulling at everything that could be pushed or pulled, checking the lights and oil. Then Doug got out a small glass bottle shaped like a test tube and pressed it up into a small hole under the wing. It half filled with fuel.

'Smell!' he said, holding the test tube out to Francesca.

Francesca frowned. 'Why?' she asked.

'Because if it doesn't smell like fuel, then it may be water,' he explained. 'The fuel tanks are in the wings and if the aircraft has been standing outside for a time, rain might get in. We do this before the first flight of the day. Look at the test tube. What can you see?'

'Nothing special,' Francesca answered, 'just clear liquid.'

'Then that's fine,' Doug went on. 'If there was water mixed in, the water would sink to the bottom and you might see a line dividing it from the fuel above.'

The checks went on for more than twenty minutes, then Doug turned to her.

'Right,' he said, 'in future you'll do all the checks on your own. As the pilot of the plane it's your responsibility to make sure it's safe to fly. Understand?'

Francesca nodded.

'OK,' he said, 'let's go flying.'

Soon they were high up above the ground, heading in the direction of the coast. The sky was especially beautiful that day: a clear blue, but dotted with clean white clouds like exploding balls of paint. Francesca began to relax. Up in the sky her fears about Doug seemed quite ridiculous. Clearly, she had got everything out of proportion.

This time they practised descending: losing height steadily using the power of the engine, holding the plane at the same angle and trying to keep the same speed. For the first few minutes, Francesca struggled, then, with her confidence returning, she began to learn the technique. After three or four attempts, she realised that a smile of success had returned to her face. Noticing this, Doug spoke.

'So, how about another go at stalling?' he said.

Francesca felt herself tense up again immediately. Would this be another opportunity for him to touch her knee? She was determined not to show her fears. 'Good,' she answered. 'I want to get that right.'

Doug gave a short laugh. 'OK, take us up to 4000 feet again and let's see what happens.'

Feeling her heart start to race, Francesca put the plane

into a climb. Once they'd reached height, they checked their safety harnesses and Francesca looked carefully all around outside the plane. Then, at Doug's instruction, she killed the power and prepared for the stall.

'Pull back ... pull back ... that's the idea.' Doug's words were more familiar this time. So, too, was the plane's behaviour. After what seemed like an age, the plane began trembling just as before, then it suddenly collapsed forward.

This time Francesca was ready for it. As the nose fell towards the ground, she pushed the control column forward and slowly increased the power. The plane responded immediately, the wings grabbing at the sky, as if it were a climber pulling itself back up a mountain.

Francesca breathed a sigh of relief. She hadn't panicked, she had overcome her fears. And Doug hadn't touched her. Everything was all right.

Doug was looking at her. 'You're a quick learner, Francesca,' he said. Then he added with a short laugh, 'Just a pity you don't need calming down.'

Chapter 5 *Getting to know you*

Ninety minutes later, Francesca was hurrying down the road to the airfield gates. The lesson had finished late and now she was in danger of missing her bus. She broke into a run. If she missed the bus, she wouldn't be back in time to get the children's dinner. But despite running the rest of the way, she saw the bus disappearing round the bend just as she reached the gates.

Miserably, she sank down onto the grass by the entrance. The next bus wasn't for another hour. She could ring Mrs Thompson, but she didn't want to let her down. She was just on the point of calling a taxi and facing up to all that expense when she saw a grey Audi approaching. The next moment it pulled up beside her. It was Doug. He lowered the window and leant across.

'Waiting for a pick-up?' he asked.

Francesca's heart missed a beat. Suddenly, she wasn't sure of her English. Didn't 'pick-up' have a double meaning?

'I missed my bus,' she answered flatly.

'Jump in,' he went on. 'I'll give you a lift.'

The passenger door opened. Francesca stood there looking at it stupidly. Half a dozen conflicting thoughts were rushing round her head, some saying: 'Don't get in, don't be crazy,' while others were saying: 'Don't be ridiculous, you've just been alone in a plane with him! What's the difference?'

'What's the problem?' Doug asked.

Taking a deep breath, Francesca stepped forward, climbed inside the car and pulled the door closed.

All of sudden she felt trapped. The car pulled away. Soon they were driving towards the city centre. Francesca tried to calm herself.

After a short time, Doug glanced across. 'So, tell me more about yourself,' he said. 'I think we ought to know a little about each other, don't you – especially if we're spending all this time alone together.'

Francesca felt her whole body tense up. 'You know most things about me already,' she murmured.

'No, I don't,' Doug answered. 'I'm interested. A beautiful girl like you, giving up everything in Switzerland and coming over here to learn to fly. Most girls your age are probably chatting on Facebook and discussing boyfriends.'

'I'm not fifteen years old,' Francesca replied sharply.

'Oh, I can see that,' Doug answered, looking across. 'No, I simply meant you're pretty unusual. Not many of my students come for their flying lessons by bus, you know.'

Francesca kept her eyes firmly on the road ahead.

'It must have meant a lot of sacrifices,' Doug said.

Feeling she had to reply, Francesca answered, 'Not many.'

'Come on,' Doug continued, 'What about holidays, clothes, all that sort of thing? And no doubt you've left behind at least one boy with an aching heart.'

Francesca felt sick. She was urging the car on, willing it to get to the city quickly.

'Why do you keep asking about boyfriends?' she said, trying to keep control of her voice.

This seemed to amuse Doug even more. 'I just thought it might be quite lonely for you here all on your own.' He looked across at her and smiled.

Francesca took a moment to reply. 'Look,' she said, unable to hide her temper. 'I don't think my private life is any of your business. But if you must know – yes, I'm on my own and I'm very happy like that. All I want to do is get my pilot's licence. Just now I'm not interested in anything else.'

'An excellent philosophy,' Doug said. He turned towards her, that familiar smile playing around his lips again. 'Apologies for asking.'

Francesca didn't look back. Her blood was still boiling. After a couple of seconds, Doug looked away again.

They drove on in silence for a couple of minutes. Then, all of a sudden, Doug turned onto a quieter road.

Francesca tensed up again. It wasn't the route the bus took. 'Where are we going?' she asked.

'I thought you lived in Eaton,' Doug said. 'This is a short cut.'

Francesca shivered. A horrible scene began playing out in her mind: Doug driving her to some secret place, locking the car doors so she was trapped inside, then forcing himself on her. Her heart raced crazily. Surely it would be madness for him to try anything? She took a deep breath.

Doug glanced round. 'Are you all right?' he asked. 'You look very pale.'

'I'm fine,' Francesca answered weakly.

Doug watched her for a second or two longer, looking unconvinced. He didn't say anything for a time. They drove on.

After a couple of turns, Francesca suddenly recognised a church on the left-hand side. She breathed a sigh of relief. Perhaps Doug had taken a short cut after all.

'What's the name of your road?' Doug asked.

Francesca hesitated. 'If you just drop me here, I'll be fine,' she said quickly.

'Don't be silly,' Doug answered. 'Considering how much you're paying me, taking you back home for once is the least I can do.'

Francesca couldn't see a way out. 'It's Brabazon Road,' she said quietly.

Doug nodded. After several more turns, they swung into Francesca's road.

'What number?' Doug asked.

'Really, just here would be great,' Francesca protested.

'I run a door-to-door service,' Doug answered firmly.

Francesca swallowed hard. 'It's the big house on the left, just after the second tree,' she said.

A couple of moments later they pulled up at the entrance to her driveway. Francesca felt relief flood through her.

'Thank you very much,' she said, feeling she should try to be polite.

'My pleasure,' Doug said, smiling.

Francesca had her hand on the door. The next moment Doug suddenly leant across her. Terrified, Francesca pressed herself back into the seat. What was happening?

Doug gave a short laugh. 'Take it easy! I'm only opening the door for you.' He stretched right across her and reached to the door. 'Handle's a bit awkward, you see.'

The door swung open. Francesca climbed out.

'Thank you again,' she said very quietly.

Doug pulled the door shut and drove off without replying.

Chapter 6 *If only …*

That evening, once Sam and Emma, the Thompson's children, had gone to bed and Francesca had cleared up in the kitchen, she went back up to her room to make her daily Skype call to her parents. As usual, she kept it cheerful and positive. She told them happily of all the progress she'd made and related a couple of Doug's comments praising her flying skills. She then concentrated on news about Sam and Emma, which was what her mother was most interested in.

With her family duty done, Francesca then decided to email Antonella, her best friend back home. Although her message was definitely still positive, she finished, 'The only problem is that the instructor, Doug, makes me feel really uncomfortable. Although he's a good pilot, he makes these weird remarks and I keep thinking he's about to make some sort of sexual move. He definitely touched my knee! He seems to be laughing at me half the time and he really scares me. I just don't like him.'

Once she'd finished her email, Francesca read it through. She stared for a long time at the lines she'd written about Doug. Finally, with a little cry of annoyance, she deleted everything she'd said about him, and pressed 'Send' before she could change her mind.

She was about to shut down the laptop, when she found herself opening up the Internet again and typing in the address of the Fastwings website. The familiar front page opened up: the picture of her Cessna, G-AZBA, Doug in flying jacket and sunglasses, leaning up against the engine.

A couple of bubbles of text near the bottom caught her eye – recommendations from previous students: 'Superb instruction from beginning to end. I never expected it to be so much fun!' And another: 'As a one-man show, Fastwings can keep costs to a minimum. Getting my licence was cheaper than I imagined!'

Francesca thought about the comments. It was that second one, emphasising how cheap it was, which had made her pick Fastwings. She wished now she'd chosen another flying school. She'd considered others at the time – there was even another one at Norwich.

She typed that in now: Flying Start. A fresh page appeared. She remembered it immediately: the rather unappealing picture of a young student sitting in the cockpit beside his instructor. The instructor looked very formal in his white shirt and tie – another reason why Francesca had chosen Fastwings. Doug had seemed so much more casual. Francesca tried to see into the Flying Start instructor's eyes. He looked very correct, certainly not someone who might try to take advantage of her.

An idea flashed through her mind. Could she switch schools, ask for her money back from Fastwings, then sign up at Flying Start? She wouldn't have to begin all over again, she would be able to continue from the point she'd already reached. But almost as quickly as the idea had come, it died. How could she ask Doug for her money back? What could she give as a reason?

Francesca closed down her computer quickly, angry with herself now. What was she thinking? Doug hadn't done anything. Well, he'd possibly touched her on the knee, but nothing more. Nothing had happened! She'd let her imagination run wild in the car with him. What was wrong with her? Perhaps living here in England all on her own was too much for her. Perhaps she was too young.

Feeling furious with herself, Francesca marched through into the bathroom, tore off her clothes and stood under the shower. Finally, after a couple of minutes under the steady stream of water, she began to calm down.

*   *   *

Francesca was determined to focus on her flying when she arrived at the airfield for her next lesson. She knocked on the office door and was surprised when a woman's voice told her to come in.

When she entered, she found a dark-haired woman of about forty, sitting on the sofa. She looked tired and fed up. Two little girls were kneeling at her feet, drawing in colouring books on the low table in front of her. Francesca recognised them from the photo on Doug's desk.

'You must be Francesca,' the woman said immediately.

Francesca realised it was Doug's wife.

'Mrs Barker?' she said.

'That's right,' the woman replied. 'I've heard all about you. Doug's star pupil!' She didn't wait for a response, but began gathering her things together. 'Don't worry, we're not staying. We just came to bring Doug his phone. He left it on the dining table. He's always forgetting things, poor man.'

Francesca didn't know how to react. The woman sounded bitter and sarcastic. Sometimes the English way of saying the opposite of what was meant left her completely confused. But she didn't need to think of an answer because the next moment Doug came in.

'Don't bother with the introductions,' Mrs Barker said, 'we've already done all that. Besides, we're going. How much did you manage to get?'

A brief discussion followed which Francesca understood was something to do with money. Doug then took out his wallet and handed across a couple of notes, which his wife immediately put in her bag.

All of a sudden, Doug marched across the room.

'I told you not to do that!' he shouted, pulling up one of the girls roughly by the arm. 'I told you not to get your pens all over the floor!'

The girl's face immediately twisted in fear and alarm. The next moment she began to cry. She ran over to her mother's side.

'Oh, brilliant work, Doug!' his wife said sharply.

'Well, it serves her right. She should bloody well listen when I give her orders,' Doug said angrily.

A short argument followed. Eventually, Doug's wife gathered the children together and they made for the door. Doug meanwhile sank down into a chair and watched the scene moodily. A moment or two later, with barely a word of goodbye, the small group hurried away.

When they'd gone, Doug twisted his face into a frown.

'See what I mean about the joys of marriage?' he said.

Francesca didn't respond.

At last Doug pulled himself upright. 'OK, "landings" today, wasn't it? Perhaps you could do me a favour and fly us straight into the ground.'

Chapter 7 *An unhappy client*

For the next half hour, Francesca listened while Doug explained in detail the principles of landing. It seemed the general idea was to bring the plane slowly down, by carefully controlling the power. The most difficult part was the final moments. When the plane was six or seven metres above the ground, you had to 'flare' – to pull back gently on the control column so that the main wheels touched the ground before the nose wheel. At that point you had to hold steady, letting the speed die away, so that the plane would gently sink down.

'It's not as easy as it sounds,' Doug added. 'Some students get it almost immediately; some take a long time. Judging when to flare – when to pull back – is the biggest problem. You have to wait until the ground seems to be rushing up to meet you … that's the moment to flare.'

By the time they got up in the air, Francesca was quite nervous. She was trying to concentrate on flying, but she couldn't stop thinking about the scene with Mrs Barker and Doug's treatment of his daughter. It had shocked her tremendously – the anger and violence hidden just beneath the surface. She wondered if this was Doug's true nature. The more she got to know him, the less she liked him.

They climbed to 1000 feet and flew down the western side of the airfield, parallel to the runway. It was windier than usual and Francesca found it difficult to control the plane; she couldn't seem to find the right power to keep the plane straight and level.

Soon they were turning back towards the airfield. The runway lay ahead in the distance. Doug began a steady stream of instructions.

'OK, reduce power,' he said. 'Hold her steady at 80. Not too slow ... keep your speed up.'

Francesca looked along the nose. The runway was creeping towards them, growing bigger all the time, but it was a little over to the left.

'Keep the plane in line with the runway!' Doug called. 'You're not on the centre line.'

Francesca tried to correct their direction, but when she did so, the nose came up.

'Watch your speed!' Doug shouted. 'You're down to 65!'

Francesca pushed in the throttle, but it was too much. Instantly, the plane rose upwards. Francesca pushed the control column forward, then at last regained control.

'Are you OK?' Doug asked, glancing across.

'I'm fine,' Francesca answered quickly.

'Right, try and keep her like this then,' he said.

Francesca's eyes flashed between the dials inside the cockpit and the runway visible above the nose.

The plane slipped slowly down towards the ground.

The runway was getting closer and closer, the black and white stripes at its end like a set of piano keys.

'Aim just beyond the piano keys,' Doug said, more gently now. 'That's good. Hold it there. Now watch for the ground rush.'

Francesca froze. What did it mean? What was the 'ground rush'? The runway already looked huge. She waited. Should she pull back now? Surely they would hit the ground at any moment!

She pulled back on the control column and at the same time reduced the power. As the nose lifted, the runway disappeared from sight. They seemed to be flying on blindly, the plane hanging in the air only a couple of metres above the ground. They held like that for an age, speed dropping, like a boat sinking in the water. Then, suddenly, there was a terrific bang. For a second, Francesca thought they'd crashed. Then she realised the main wheels had hit the ground.

'OK, push the control column forward slowly to bring down the nose wheel,' Doug called.

Francesca obeyed automatically. She watched the nose slowly drop, then felt the front wheel touch the ground. The plane rolled steadily forward, eventually coming to a stop.

'All right, take her off the runway,' Doug instructed. 'Then let's have a talk.'

Francesca did as she was told. She felt suddenly hot and embarrassed; the headphones were tight on her ears.

'OK, stop here,' Doug said.

Francesca brought the plane to a stop. She felt afraid of what Doug was going to say; the landing had been so heavy.

'Have I damaged the plane?' she began. 'There was so much to think about. I didn't expect …'

'Don't worry about it,' Doug interrupted. He turned towards Francesca and looked at her closely. 'Heavy landings are quite normal at this stage. But you're not concentrating today. There's something on your mind.'

Francesca blinked. Was it really so obvious? She didn't know what to say.

'I … I didn't sleep well last night. Maybe that's it,' she said a bit desperately.

Doug raised his eyebrows. He kept his eyes on her. 'I hope you're happy with the lessons,' he went on quietly.

Francesca felt completely frozen: the harness trapping her back against the seat, the cockpit tinier than ever. 'Of course,' she lied.

Doug continued to watch her. Then, keeping his eyes on her all the time, he stretched out his hand and placed it on top of hers where she was resting it on her knees.

'Good,' he said, squeezing her hand very gently. 'Because I'm very happy with you.'

Francesca didn't move. Doug's words seemed to hang in the cockpit. She felt suddenly sick. The image of a huge fleshy spider resting on the back of her hand flashed into her mind.

After a moment or two more, Doug took his hand away.

'Right, turn the aircraft round and take her back to the runway,' he said. 'Let's see if we can get these landings sorted out today.'

Francesca was still frozen. Although Doug had removed his hand, it still felt as though there was a spider resting on hers. She had to look to check there wasn't one there.

'OK, let's go,' Doug said.

Francesca tried to refocus on flying. She reached forward to the throttle and pushed it in to increase the power. The plane leapt forward fast, too fast. Immediately, she pulled at the control column.

'Whoah!' Doug called. 'We don't want to take off!' Using his controls, he brought the plane to a stop.

Francesca closed her eyes. She felt her arms shaking slightly as she held the control column. She was sure it must be noticeable.

All of a sudden she felt a hand on her leg.

Francesca's eyes shot open. She looked down to see the man squeezing the top of her leg gently.

'Take your hand off me!' she shouted.

Doug smiled at her across the cockpit. 'Whatever you say,' he said casually and slowly removed his hand. 'Shame,' he added more quietly. 'I guess we'd better concentrate on these landings.'

All of a sudden Francesca knew she couldn't go on. 'I want to stop. I want to stop the lesson,' Francesca said quickly. 'I don't feel very well.'

Doug looked across and raised his eyebrows. For a moment she thought he was going to lean across and try to kiss her, and she froze. Then, with heavy sarcasm, he said. 'As you wish. Don't want an unhappy client, do we?'

Francesca didn't reply.

Doug took over the controls and took the plane back towards the hangar without speaking.

Chapter 8 *Coffee break*

When Francesca marched out of the Fastwings office that afternoon, she had just missed one bus into the city and it was almost a two-hour wait till the next. She didn't care. It was just a relief to be out of the place and away from Doug. For fifteen minutes she walked as fast as she could, going wherever her footsteps took her, dragging her hand through her hair, as if by doing so she might empty her head of the memory of Doug's hand on hers – the imaginary spider. When she had at last calmed down, she found she had walked right round to the other side of the airfield.

As she was walking back towards the airfield gates, a sign on the hangar she was passing caught her eye. 'Flying Start: Pilot Training,' it read – it was the other flying school she'd been looking at online the night before.

A small door was cut into the hangar wall. Perhaps if it hadn't been open, Francesca wouldn't have thought to go and look any closer. But as it was, she wandered across and looked through the doorway. There was little light inside, but she could make out the shape of several aircraft in the darkness.

Without thinking, Francesca stepped inside and began making her way around the planes. They were parked tightly together, wings almost touching. Slowly, she made her way among them, studying them as if she were looking at pictures in an art gallery. Towards the back she saw an ancient yellow plane, but behind that, the shape of an expensive executive jet caught her eye. She went over to look at it more closely, admiring the smart green and gold paintwork, and the eager hungry shape of its nose.

'Beautiful, isn't she?' a voice behind her said.

Francesca swung round. A young man of about twenty-five, with longish brown hair and wearing blue work clothes, approached. He bent his head to pass under a wing, wiping his hands on an oily cloth.

'I'm sorry,' Francesca began. 'I didn't realise there was anyone here,' she added, noticing now a light aircraft behind him, its engine cover open. 'The door was open, so I ...'

'No problem,' the man replied. 'As long as you weren't planning to steal one!' Then, pointing at the jet, he went on, 'Yes, she belongs to Harry Moore – you know, the furniture man. Uses it to pop around Europe and check that everyone's making him lots of money.'

Francesca smiled. She had no idea who Harry Moore was. But this young man had a friendly and amusing way of speaking. And he looked funny. He had a big nose and there was a big black mark down the side of it, where he must have rubbed oil from his hand.

'Anyway,' he went on, 'can I help? You're not interested in flying lessons, are you?'

Francesca felt embarrassed. 'Well, umm ... actually I'm already having lessons. To be honest I'm just – how do you say? – killing time.' She was about to explain about the bus when the man broke in.

'Oh, hold on a minute. You must be Doug's Swiss-Italian, is that right?' he asked, then cut himself short. 'Oh dear, that doesn't sound very good, does it? I'm really sorry; I just heard someone say Doug had a foreign student taking flying lessons. You're quite famous, you know.'

Francesca wasn't sure she liked this idea. But there was something light and easy about the man's way of speaking, and he'd made a funny face at his mistake which relaxed her immediately. After all the tension of the afternoon it was a wonderful relief.

'Do you work for Flying Start?' she asked.

'Yes,' the man answered. 'I'm the office manager.' He smiled. 'Big title, small job – I answer the phone and help maintain the aircraft and so on. Tom Brennan's the name,' he said. As he did so, he put out his hand, then realising it was covered in oil, took it back, smiling.

'Sorry, probably not such a good idea.'

Francesca laughed. 'No problem. And I'm Francesca Bartolli,' she said.

'Nice to meet you,' he said.

Francesca smiled. 'Good to meet you, too,' she said.

They looked at each other for a second or two, uncertain how to continue, then Tom went on. 'I don't suppose you fancy a cup of coffee, do you? I'm just about to make one.'

Francesca hesitated. 'Aren't you busy?' she asked.

'I was about to have a break anyway,' Tom said. 'I'll just go and wash my hands.'

Tom led the way round the planes and out of the hangar into a small office. Over to one side there was a small sofa and a table covered in flying magazines. Leaving her there, Tom went off to the washroom. A few minutes later, he reappeared, carrying two cups of steaming coffee.

'There,' he said. 'Not exactly café latte, but at least it's hot and wet.'

When she tasted the coffee, Francesca realised the man hadn't been joking – it was awful. But she didn't care; it was just such a relaxing atmosphere after being with Doug. 'It's drinkable,' she said with a smile.

Tom laughed and sat down beside the desk. 'So,' he began, 'how are your lessons going?'

'Not too badly, I think,' Francesca answered. 'I didn't do very well today though. I made quite a mess of my first landing.'

Tom grinned. 'You're alive, aren't you? You know the definition of a good landing?' he asked. 'One that you are able to walk away from.'

Francesca laughed.

Tom went on. 'So, why do you want to learn to fly?' he asked lightly.

'I want to be a commercial pilot,' Francesca answered.

Tom sat up in surprise. 'Wow!' he said. 'Good for you! I'm impressed. So why are you learning here? Not enough flat land back home in Switzerland?'

Francesca laughed again and explained all about it. Tom listened carefully. Soon Francesca realised she'd told him all about her family and home and then they'd moved on to discuss all things Swiss and Italian: the people and food, even the Italian language. Twenty minutes had passed before she knew it.

'And what about you?' Francesca asked the moment there was a break in the conversation. 'I suppose you got your pilot's licence years ago.'

'Actually, no,' Tom replied. 'My father was a pilot in the Royal Air Force – and thought I'd be brilliant, but to be perfectly honest, I didn't enjoy it much. Got in a total panic and scared the instructor out of his pants. I'm happier on the ground. But I still think planes are very beautiful.'

'Yes, I know what you mean. My friends all thought I was crazy when I said that,' she replied, happy to have found someone who felt the same.

They fell silent for a moment and she suddenly began to wonder if she'd stayed too long.

'I'm sorry,' she said. 'I ought to go and let you get on with your work.'

Tom gave a small smile. 'Yes, I suppose so,' he said uncertainly. 'The boss will be back soon.'

Francesca felt awkward. They both stood up, a bit embarrassed.

As Francesca got to her feet, she noticed the drawing of a bird – an owl – on a notepad on the desk. It was beautiful: detailed and delicate.

Tom saw her looking at it. 'The head's not quite right,' he said. 'I've got to do that bit again.'

'You drew it?' Francesca asked. 'But it's lovely!' she went on, genuinely impressed. 'It must have taken ages.'

'About half an hour,' Tom replied. 'Sometimes there isn't a lot to do in the office,' he added with a laugh.

Francesca studied it carefully. 'It's fantastic,' she said at last. 'Do you draw other things as well as birds?'

'Well, people sometimes,' he answered. 'But mostly birds and planes. Anything that flies, I suppose.'

'You've got a real talent,' Francesca said.

Tom looked a bit embarrassed. Then, all of a sudden, he tore off the sheet with the bird and handed it to Francesca.

'Here,' he said. 'A small gift.'

Francesca protested only briefly before accepting the drawing.

Tom showed her out of the hangar.

'Well, good luck with your flying lessons,' he said once they were outside. 'Doug's certainly a brilliant pilot, or so I've heard.'

Francesca's heart sank. For the last half-hour, she'd forgotten all about Doug. She didn't say anything.

'Drop in again next time you're here,' Tom said suddenly. 'I'm nearly always around if you fancy another coffee.'

Francesca smiled and put out her hand. Their eyes met for a second. She wondered if she would see Tom again. Then she set off down the path towards the airfield gates.

When she'd gone ten metres or so, she couldn't help glancing round. Tom was still standing in the doorway. With a little wave, he immediately disappeared back into the office.

Chapter 9   *A difficult phone call*

As soon as she'd put Sam and Emma to bed that evening, Francesca hurried up the stairs to her room, turned on her laptop, and opened up the Flying Start website.

Reading through all the details now, she couldn't understand why she'd ever chosen Fastwings. Flying Start had more aircraft, more instructors, and offered several more courses. Besides that, now she examined the website more closely, the whole place seemed more attractive. In a section called 'Gallery' there was a huge display of photos: aircraft in flight, aircraft on the ground, sunlit landscapes taken from the air, the same scenes repeated with snow on the ground. Francesca looked at them, feeling increasingly annoyed, unable to believe that she'd ignored them before.

There was another section called 'Staff'. This time she checked the photos more carefully: there seemed to be three main instructors – two youngish men: Nick Downing and Brian Hamilton, and a much older man, George Scott. Next, there was a photo of Tom. Francesca looked at it for a long time. It was unmistakeably him – the nose was so recognisable. He was standing beside one of the aircraft, smiling shyly. He looked kind and honest, his eyes wide and warm. Had she really seen the photograph before? She couldn't remember it and felt slightly ashamed at the thought. She glanced at the drawing of the owl that she'd already put on the noticeboard above her desk. If only she had taken up lessons at Flying Start! But she'd paid for the whole private pilot's licence course with Doug; she was committed to lessons with him. The memory of his hand on her hand and leg came flooding back. She could feel it even now – like a huge great tarantula creeping up her body. It made her feel sick; it made her want to scream!

Quite why she didn't close down the laptop at that moment, she never fully understood. Later, she wished she had just shut it down and gone to bed. But after hesitating for a few seconds, she did a search for Doug by typing in his name. Instantly, half a dozen 'Doug Barkers' appeared with Facebook entries. She quickly checked the photos one by one, but they were clearly not the Doug she knew. Next she tried 'Doug Barker Flying Instructor'. This time the results were different. An entry half the way down the page caught her eye. 'Flying instructor wins damages' it read. It appeared to be from a newspaper, *The Southampton Herald*.

With a feeling of sickness about what she might discover, Francesca opened the page and saw a photo of the Doug Barker she knew only too well. He was standing beside an aircraft, hand on its nose. Below the photograph, was a report. With increasing horror, Francesca read:

A Southampton flying instructor yesterday won damages against a woman who had accused him of sexual harassment. The woman, who remains unnamed, had accused Doug Barker, 37, of making sexual advances to her while she was receiving flying lessons from him. The woman yesterday admitted in court that she was unable to provide evidence and all charges against Mr Barker were dropped. The judge ordered the woman to pay Barker £2500 in damages …

It was a very long time before Francesca got to sleep that night.

* * *

At ten o'clock the next morning, Francesca, sat down at the desk in her room, and picked up her mobile phone. After closing her eyes for a second or two, she searched down through the numbers until she found the one for Fastwings. Then, before she could change her mind, she pressed the Call button.

The number rang for a very long time. Half of Francesca was praying that it wouldn't be answered, but just as she was about to give up, she heard Doug's voice.

'Fastwings,' was all he said.

Francesca decided she must sound firm. Taking a deep breath, she said, 'Hello, it's Francesca here … Francesca Bartolli.'

Doug gave a short cruel laugh. 'Ah, Francesca *Bartolli*,' he responded sarcastically. 'For a moment, I thought it might be the other Francesca I teach.'

Francesca didn't respond. She hated Doug now; hated him with all her heart.

'So, what can I do for Francesca?' he asked.

Francesca took another deep breath. 'I'm ringing,' she said, 'because I've decided I must cancel.'

There was a slight pause. Then Doug spoke again. 'I see,' he said carefully. 'When would you like your lesson instead?'

Francesca put a hand to her head. 'No,' she said more quietly. 'I mean I want to cancel the course. I've decided not to continue the flying lessons.'

There was a long silence after that. Francesca's hand trembled as she waited for Doug's response. The silence went on and on. Finally, Francesca decided something must be wrong.

'Are you still there?' she asked.

'Oh yes, I'm here,' Doug replied.

He didn't say anything more. Francesca felt a tight ball in her throat.

At last Doug broke the silence. 'What's the problem, Francesca?' he asked. 'Just because I put my hand on you a couple of times to calm you down … Is that really so terrible?'

'It wasn't to calm me down,' she replied quickly.

'What was it then?' Doug asked.

'You know very well,' she protested. 'But it's not only that – it's …' She stopped. Francesca didn't know what to say. She didn't want to say anything about what she'd read the previous night. She bit her lip.

'What exactly are you accusing me of, Francesca?' Doug asked quietly.

Francesca searched for words. She'd prepared in advance what she was going to say, but now the memory of that newspaper article had wiped all the words from her head.

'I … I just want to stop,' Francesca said, her nerve failing her. 'I can't explain. I'm sorry. It was a mistake.'

After another pause, Doug spoke again. 'I see,' he said. 'So you're not going to have lessons somewhere else then?'

Francesca hesitated. Although she'd expected the question, now she realised she had made the mistake of not deciding firmly on the answer.

'I haven't made any plans,' she said. 'I'm not sure. I may go back to Switzerland.' It came out before she knew she was going to say it.

'What a pity,' Doug replied, with a hint of sarcasm.

'Yes,' Francesca said.

There was another silence.

'Well, don't expect any of your money back,' Doug said finally.

'What do you mean?' Francesca asked. 'You can't keep my money!'

There was a pause. Then Doug spoke again. 'I don't know about that, Francesca. You see, the way I understand it, we had a contract – a contract for a whole flying course, and now you're trying to break the contract. I think I can do whatever I like and you don't have a leg to stand on.'

Francesca felt panic rising suddenly in her throat. 'I … I don't understand. What do you mean, "a leg to stand on"?'

'I mean, you can't do anything about it, Francesca,' Doug answered slowly. 'If I decide not to give you any money back, then that's your hard luck.'

Francesca didn't know what to do. She could hardly breathe.

'But you can't do that!' she said.

'Listen, Ms Bartolli,' Doug replied with exaggerated politeness. 'You've called to tell me you want to break your contract and as good as accused me of trying to rape you! How do expect me to react? Who exactly do you think you are? It seems to me you've got a pretty big idea of yourself!'

Francesca felt tears coming and it made her furious. She never cried. She didn't know what to do, what to say. Suddenly she felt completely out of her depth.

'Please,' she said desperately, hating herself for being weak. 'Don't do this to me!'

There was another pause.

'Well, I'll have to think about it. You say you're going back to Switzerland?'

Francesca fought against the tears.

'Probably,' she muttered.

'Because if you decide to join another flying school here, I will be very, very angry,' he went on.

Francesca felt the tears rising up through her body and all of a sudden, just as they burst, she shouted out down the phone.

'Oh, stop it, please! Just leave me alone!' Then, without knowing she was about to say it, she added, 'I wish I'd never come here. I hate it here in England. I just want to go home!'

With that, she ended the call and in a sudden fit of despair, threw the phone hard down onto her bed. It bounced once, and crashed against the wall. As the flood of tears streamed from her eyes, Francesca saw that the phone had broken open and the battery had fallen onto the floor. She threw herself onto the bed and covered her head with the pillow.

Chapter 10 *A fresh start*

'I don't understand why you have to leave,' Sam said bitterly, kicking his heels against the park bench. 'I don't want you to go back to Switzerland.'

Francesca gave a deep sigh. It was over a week later and she was sitting in the park near the Thompson's house, watching the children play in the warm May sunshine. After playing on the swings for a good while, Sam had come over and sunk down beside Francesca, exhausted.

'I'm sorry, Sam,' Francesca began. 'It's very difficult to explain, but I've had to change my plans.'

'But why?' the little boy asked.

'Because … because things haven't worked out the way I'd hoped,' Francesca answered.

'But you said you were going to be a pilot,' Sam said with a frown. 'You said you were going to fly planes!'

Francesca dropped her head. Mrs Thompson had warned Francesca how upset the children would be. Sam was such a sweet little boy and she loved him dearly, but she wished he would stop. Making the decision to go home to Switzerland had been terrible enough. Now, if the children were going to question her in this way, it would be unbearable.

Francesca had told Mrs Thompson of her decision the day after the phone call to Doug. Mrs Thompson had been quite disappointed herself. 'Oh no, not really?' she'd said. 'But I thought you were enjoying it here. And you seemed to be doing so well with the flying lessons!'

Francesca hadn't known what to say. For some reason she didn't want to tell Mrs Thompson about Doug's behaviour or what she'd read. She didn't want to tell anyone. She couldn't properly understand it herself, but she felt strangely ashamed – as though she was partly responsible for what had happened.

Instead, she told Mrs Thompson that taking flying lessons in a foreign language had proved to be more difficult than she'd realised at the beginning. Francesca guessed that Mrs Thompson hadn't really believed it. But the woman was sensitive enough not to press Francesca for any further explanation. She simply said how sorry she was, and how sorry the children would be to see her go. Francesca's departure was set for a month's time – the period of notice she was obliged to give according to her contract.

Doug's threat not to return the money for the unused lessons had also dominated Francesca's thoughts all week. As each day passed her anxiety grew, until finally Mrs Thompson asked what was worrying her so much.

Francesca explained what Doug had said about her breaking the contract and losing her money. Mrs Thompson was shocked and that night told her husband, who was a solicitor. Mr Thompson took one look at the paperwork Francesca had received from Fastwings, and said, 'The man's talking rubbish! What's the telephone number of this place?'

Francesca didn't hear the phone call, but a short while later Mr Thompson appeared saying, 'What a thoroughly unpleasant man. I think you're better off having nothing more to do with him!' Two days later, a cheque had arrived in the post.

The sound of someone calling her name brought Francesca back to the present and made her look up. A cyclist had stopped about ten metres away and was calling across.

'Francesca? Yes, it is!'

Francesca stared for a moment, still lost in her thoughts, then realised who it was. The man was already wheeling his bike towards her.

'Do you remember me? Tom Brennan ... from Flying Start?'

Francesca blinked a couple of times. 'But, of course I do,' she answered. 'Nice to see you again,' she said, genuinely pleased to see a friendly face.

'Great to see you, too,' Tom said. 'How are you? How are things?'

Francesca paused for a moment before replying, wondering what to tell him. But there was no point in going into the whole business with Doug.

'I'm fine,' she said, as Sam went running off back to the swings. Then, she went on quickly: 'How about you?'

'Oh, same as ever,' Tom answered. He went on immediately: 'Seeing you here is really funny because I was thinking about you only yesterday.'

Francesca frowned, not quite sure what was coming next.

'Yeah, you see I noticed there was a new film out at the cinema, a film about Amelia Earhart, you know—'

Francesca interrupted him: 'Yes, the first woman to fly across the Atlantic.'

'That's right,' he went on. 'Anyway, I just thought ...' He seemed to lose confidence all of a sudden. 'Well, I just wondered if you'd like to see it ... if you're not busy, that is.'

Francesca's heart gave a little leap, excited at the thought. But then, just as quickly, her heart fell. She was leaving for Switzerland in less than a month. What was the point of getting to know him better? It was just stupid and unfair.

Tom misunderstood Francesca's silence.

'Sorry,' Tom went on, rubbing the side of his nose all of a sudden. 'I just thought that as it was a film about flying and a famous woman pilot, you might …'

'Oh, I'd love to it see it,' Francesca said looking him directly in the eyes, 'and I really appreciate you asking, but there's something you should know.'

'You've got a boyfriend …' Tom said.

Francesca took a breath. 'No, no, it's not that. The fact is I'm going back to Switzerland in three weeks' time.'

'What!' Tom said.

'Yes, I decided …' Francesca paused.

'Why?' Tom asked, concerned. 'What's happened?'

Francesca thought about the excuse she'd given Mrs Thompson. But for some reason the words seemed to stick in her throat.

Tom broke in, embarrassed. 'I'm sorry. It's none of my business, but I'd heard you were doing brilliantly at Fastwings,' Tom said. 'You were getting on well with Doug—'

'I wasn't,' Francesca cut in.

'Sorry?'

'I wasn't getting on with him at all,' Francesca answered, strangely relieved to have told him the truth.

'Why?' Tom answered, clearly very surprised.

'I don't want to go into the reasons,' Francesca said quickly. 'I just don't like him, that's all. He wasn't very nice to me and I don't like the way he treats his children either. He frightens me, actually.'

'Oh …' Tom answered, trying to absorb what he'd just heard. 'I must say I'd heard Doug could be quite a hard instructor. And I think he's going through a bit of a bad time just now,' he added. 'All the same …'

'What do you mean?' Francesca asked. 'What kind of bad time?'

'Oh, I don't know,' Tom answered. 'Financial problems, I think. Apparently he borrowed a lot of money to set up Fastwings. And personal things, as well. There's a rumour his marriage is on the rocks, actually.'

Francesca was silent for a moment. The idea of the man's private life collapsing would only make him more unstable and it frightened her more than ever.

'But anyway, that's no reason for you to stop your lessons,' Tom went on, interrupting her thoughts. 'You've come this far – you simply mustn't give up. Come and have a try at Flying Start. We'd love to have you.'

'I'm sorry, Tom,' Francesca said. 'Something's happened. I've lost my confidence, I think …'

'What! I can't believe that,' Tom protested.

'I can't carry on, Tom,' she said. 'I feel a complete mess. Besides, Doug would be furious if he knew I was starting lessons with you.'

'Well, that's his problem. Anyway, you don't have to tell him you're flying with us,' Tom answered.

'He'll kill me if he finds out,' Francesca murmured.

'Rubbish,' Tom answered. 'Anyway, I'm not going to let you run off to Switzerland. Make a fresh start! I absolutely insist. When are you free next?'

Chapter 11   *A gentle touch*

That night, lying there in the darkness, Francesca replayed her meeting with Tom over and over in her mind. It was amazing to her how quickly and dramatically her mood could change. All the previous week she'd been down in the deepest depths of misery, her dream of becoming a pilot completely ruined. Then, all of a sudden, after meeting Tom in the park, she was sailing up through the clouds, floating through the air like a bubble of soap. It made her want to laugh; she actually lay there on the pillow with a smile on her lips. Life could begin again! The dream was not dead.

As she finally drifted closer to sleep, the memory of Tom's face formed in her mind. She liked his big nose. It made her smile once again to remember the way he kept holding it between his thumb and finger, as if hoping to find that it might have reduced in size.

*   *   *

It was a long wait till her next free afternoon, but the following Tuesday, she was waiting at her window when Tom's small red car pulled into the Thompson's driveway. Telling herself not to rush and seem too eager, she waited until she saw him climb out of the car and approach the front door. Then she ran down the stairs and opened the door.

'Hi,' he said cheerfully, touching his nose as he did so. Francesca couldn't prevent a small laugh. Tom looked puzzled.

'What's funny?' he asked.

'Nothing. I'm sorry, I'm just excited,' Francesca replied.

They stood there, looking at one another for a moment or two, both a little embarrassed, then Tom laughed as well.

'Right, we'd better go!'

They climbed in the car and set off, still laughing, like over-excited children. Soon, they were speeding towards the airfield. Tom proved to be a terrible driver – either that or his nerves had got the better of him. They seemed to approach traffic lights and roundabouts at great speed, then need to brake very hard. At the same time, Tom chatted away happily, telling Francesca all about Flying Start and its history, about the aircraft and about George, the instructor who would take her flying that afternoon. Francesca could hardly take a word in. She was so excited, so relieved that her life was moving forward again. She sat back with her head close to the open window and let the wind blow through her hair. She felt as though she'd been reborn.

After twenty minutes they arrived at the airfield. When they went into the Flying Start office, two middle-aged men were sitting at a small round table, examining a map. Tom introduced them: Mike, another student like herself, and John, his instructor. Francesca then noticed a silver-haired man of about sixty-five sitting on the sofa, reading the newspaper and drinking coffee. For a second or two, Francesca wondered what he was doing there, but then the man got to his feet and stretched out his hand.

'Something tells me you must be Francesca,' he said. 'My name's George Scott. I believe we're going flying together.'

The moment she shook his hand, Francesca felt herself relax.

'If you're Italian, you must like coffee,' he said.

'I love coffee,' Francesca replied, a little puzzled by the man's remark.

George's eyes twinkled with amusement. 'In that case,' he went on, looking down at the cup he was holding, 'don't drink any of this stuff – unless you've got a death wish, that is.'

*   *   *

Half an hour later, after doing all the usual checks, Francesca watched from the left-hand seat of the Flying Start Cessna 152, as George climbed painfully into the plane.

'I'm getting too old for this,' George said. 'You know the worst thing about flying a light aircraft?' he went on, pulling himself up and round into the seat.

'No,' Francesca answered.

'It's getting inside the bloody plane,' George went on. He finally managed to drag his second leg inside the door, then spent another exhausting minute putting on his safety harness. Once that was done, he turned to Francesca.

'Right, take her away, Ms Bartolli. Wake me when we get to 1000 feet.'

Francesca laughed, but George was almost true to his word. For the next fifteen minutes, Francesca was totally in control and George sat beside her without saying a thing.

She took the plane round to the waiting point before the start of the runway, performed all the aircraft checks, then called to the control tower to line up on the runway. With a wave of his hand, George then indicated that she should pull forward onto the runway.

Once the control tower had cleared her for take-off, Francesca turned to him.

'Shall I take off?' she asked.

'Can't think of another way to get to 1000 feet, can you?' George replied, his eyes twinkling with good humour again.

Francesca laughed, and pushed in the throttle.

The little plane seemed to sit up suddenly, then pulled itself down the runway, gathering speed all the time. Checking the airspeed dial, Francesca watched as the needle reached 60, then she pulled back gently on the control column. Out of the corner of her eye, she was aware of George sitting up more alertly, his hands loose on his knees, ready if necessary to reach out to the controls.

They climbed steadily to height. When Francesca glanced across, she saw George searching the sky around them, checking for danger. She realised now that his casual act was exactly that. Every moment they'd been in the air he'd been ready to take control. It comforted her tremendously. While he left her to fly the plane, she felt confident that he would react quickly the moment there was a problem.

'Very nice,' he said at last. 'You've got a very gentle touch. Now, do you fancy having another go at landing? I think you said that was the point you reached at Fastwings.'

Francesca nodded. 'OK,' she answered, trying to sound positive.

They flew back along the side of the airfield. A minute later, Francesca looked over her shoulder and saw the end of the runway about forty-five degrees behind. Careful not to lose any height, she turned the plane through ninety degrees, then reduced the power a little. Slowly, they began to lose height. Half a minute later, with the end of the runway almost directly opposite the left-hand window, she turned again so the runway was directly ahead.

With her hand on the throttle, Francesca let the plane slip slowly down through the air. It was like being on a very gentle children's slide. Beside her, Francesca could see George sitting relaxed. The runway seemed to rise up to meet them. She tried to picture the moment to pull back on the control column, the rush as the ground seemed to swallow them up. 'Wait …' she murmured to herself, 'Wait …'

All of a sudden the runway seemed to open out as if it were a sheet being unfolded in front of her. She pulled back and held steady. 'Now, hold on!' she said under her breath. The plane sank gently down, then a moment later there was a small bump as the main wheels met the ground.

Carefully, she pushed the control column forward to bring the nose wheel down and they rolled along the runway. As they did so, Francesca felt the blood begin flowing back to her fingers. She hadn't realised she had been so tense.

'That, Ms Bartolli,' George said, looking across at her, 'was a landing I would have been proud of myself.'

He stretched out his hand. Smiling with delight, Francesca shook it.

Tom was waiting when they pulled up outside the hangar.

'How did it go?' he asked anxiously, as they climbed out of the plane.

'Bloody awful,' George answered, his eyes twinkling once more. 'Don't know where to start.'

'Really?' Tom said, his face screwing up.

Francesca went up to him. 'It was wonderful,' she said. 'Thank you, Tom,' she added. 'I'm *so* very glad you spotted me that afternoon in the park.'

Chapter 12 *Alone at last*

That night Francesca had to babysit, but the following evening Tom picked her up at seven thirty and they headed out to the cinema.

Tom was very gentlemanly, hurrying to open the car door for her, insisting on paying for the tickets, and buying popcorn. Francesca loved it. Her old boyfriend, Andrea, had always said such old-fashioned manners were 'uncool', but Francesca enjoyed Tom's attention. She felt very special, and it made her feel attractive; she realised now how much Andrea had taken her for granted.

Francesca loved the film. Amelia Earhart had been one of her childhood heroes and she was an interesting character in herself, quite apart from her flying achievements. As they left the cinema, Francesca felt so happy she reached out and took Tom's hand. Squeezing it excitedly, she said,

'Come on, let's go and get a drink.'

Tom's reaction to the gesture was one of almost complete astonishment, but he certainly didn't protest. Francesca was almost as astonished as Tom at what she'd done – all the emotions of the last week had left her head spinning.

When they'd found a pub and settled in a quiet corner, they chatted about the film for a time. Then Francesca said, 'Do you know, my last boyfriend would never have taken me to a film like that.'

'Why ever not?' Tom asked.

'He could never understand why I loved planes so much,' Francesca answered. 'He seemed to find it embarrassing. I think he believed a girl who liked aircraft must be strange in the head. He hated it whenever I said I wanted to become a pilot.'

Tom shook his head. 'That's crazy,' he said. 'I think it's a brilliant idea.'

Francesca nodded, delighted to find someone who thought as she did. 'Anyway,' she went on, 'I want to know more about you. You've hardly told me a thing about yourself.'

Tom gave a weak smile. 'What do you want to know?' he asked.

'Well, what are you interested in for a start?' Francesca replied.

Tom hesitated. 'Well, painting and drawing, above all. Like I said before, mostly anything that flies.'

'Would you show me your pictures some time?'

Tom looked uncomfortable. 'They're nothing special. "Traditional and unimaginative" was how they've been described,' he said.

'What do you mean?' Francesca asked.

'I went to art college after I left school,' Tom replied, then went on quite bitterly. 'They didn't much like the sort of thing I do and I didn't like their ideas, so we had a bit of an argument. I left after a couple of terms.'

'That sounds like a true artist,' Francesca replied. 'Good for you!'

Tom looked surprised. 'That's not what my father said,' Tom added. 'He called it "dropping out".'

'Well, if that bird you drew is anything to go by, it was the art college that lost out.'

'That's not quite how my father sees it,' Tom muttered. 'I've never been quite the son he wanted, I guess.'

Sensing it was a bit of a delicate area, Francesca asked him about other things and soon the subject was forgotten. Tom relaxed again. Three-quarters of an hour passed before they knew it; all of a sudden the pub was closing.

They drove back to the Thompson's, both curiously silent, a little uncertain of what lay ahead. When they reached the house, Tom pulled up beside the pavement. With the engine still running, he turned towards Francesca.

'Thank you for a wonderful evening,' he said. 'I've enjoyed it so much.'

'No, Tom, I've got to thank you,' Francesca replied. 'It was really lovely.'

They looked at each other a bit awkwardly.

After a moment Tom spoke again. 'So, I'll see you up at the airfield next Tuesday?'

'You bet,' Francesca replied. The awkwardness grew again. This time Francesca reached out her hand.

'Tom,' she said, touching him on the arm. 'I didn't thank you properly yesterday afternoon for persuading me to join Flying Start.'

'Of course, you did,' Tom protested.

'No, Tom, really,' Francesca insisted. 'Three days ago I was more depressed than I can tell you. I was about to go back to Switzerland and drop the whole idea of flying, a dream I've had since I was just a child. And then meeting you in the park ... well, you rescued me, don't you understand?'

Tom blinked in confusion. 'Really?' he asked.

'Really,' Francesca replied.

With that, she leant across the car very quickly and kissed Tom on the cheek. 'Thank you,' she said, then climbed hurriedly out of the car.

Later that night, she lay in bed thinking over her evening with Tom. It occurred to her that kissing him like that wasn't exactly the act of someone determined to avoid a relationship, but she didn't really care. There was something about his shyness that she liked and the way he seemed so proud to be with her. When she'd got out of the car after the kiss, he'd looked as wide-eyed as a young boy with a brilliant birthday gift. The memory left her with a smile as she drifted off to sleep.

*   *   *

Francesca didn't have any time off in the next few days, so she didn't see Tom again until the next Tuesday afternoon. Of course, they phoned and texted one another a number of times. When she arrived at the airfield, however, George was keen to get going quickly, so there was no time to talk.

Once Francesca had checked the aircraft, she climbed inside and started up the engine. A couple of minutes later, George pulled himself slowly into the right-hand seat.

'OK,' he said, once they were settled. 'Today I want three more landings exactly like the one you did last Thursday. Do you think you can manage that?'

They approached the runway, then waited for another plane to land. As it got nearer, Francesca recognised the Fastwings Cessna and her heart missed a beat. Although she knew Doug couldn't possibly see her, she felt herself slide lower in the seat as he flew past. When his plane had cleared the runway, they moved forward themselves and quickly took off.

A couple of minutes later they were at 1000 feet and turning round on the familiar route to land back at the airfield.

Francesca's first landing was good – not as good as the one on Thursday, but in George's words, 'quite acceptable'.

The second was brilliant. As she brought the plane down, she knew even before the wheels touched the ground, that they would just kiss the runway as softly as a pair of lips.

George was impressed. 'Very good,' he said. 'Now, pull up just there on the left.'

Francesca frowned, but did as George instructed. She felt a little disappointed. 'I thought you said we were going to do three landings,' she said, bringing the plane to a stop.

'I'm not,' George replied. 'But you are.'

George was already opening the door before she'd understood what he meant.

'You mean I'm going on my own?' she said.

'We call it "going solo",' George answered. 'Now listen. Just take the aircraft round to the start of the runway, radio the control tower for permission to take off, and take her up. Do exactly what you've just done. Just one landing, then bring her back to the hangar. All right?'

Francesca was too taken aback to protest. She nodded silently. George was already climbing out of the plane. She couldn't believe what was happening. She'd imagined that flying solo would be months ahead, after dozens and dozens of landings.

'You'll find she'll climb much quicker with only one person,' George said, already standing down on the ground.

Again, Francesca nodded.

'Away you go then,' George said. He gave an encouraging thumbs-up sign, then shut the door. The next moment he was moving away below the wing, and heading for the grass.

All of a sudden, Francesca found herself on her own. She blinked a couple of times, trying to focus. The cockpit seemed terribly empty without George close at her side. She hesitated. 'Well, this is what you wanted, isn't it?' she thought, suddenly angry with herself.

With that, she sat up, reached for the throttle and released the brakes. The plane edged forward. Through the side window she saw George making his way across the grass; he didn't turn and wave.

Francesca took the plane up to the waiting point before the runway and stopped. Clearing her throat, she called the control tower.

'Golf Lima Yankee is ready for take-off,' she said, surprised at the firmness of her voice.

'Golf Lima Yankee, you are cleared for take-off,' came the reply.

Francesca steered the plane round onto the piano keys and stopped again, the runway stretching ahead.

'This is it,' she thought. 'This is the last chance to turn back.'

She only hesitated to check all the dials and controls. Then, emptying her mind of all other thoughts, she pushed in the throttle. The plane sat up eagerly and moved forward. This time the speed picked up much faster. Soon they were at 55, and then before she knew it the nose was lifting up and they were in the air. 'Keep the nose down,' she kept telling herself. 'Don't try to climb too fast!'

George was absolutely right. Without his extra weight, the plane was up to 1000 feet in half the time it had previously taken. Steadily, Francesca turned the aircraft. As she did so, a wonderful feeling ran through her. This was it! She was solo! All those hours of work and saving had finally paid off. A smile began to creep across her face; but the moment she felt it, she wiped it away. 'Francesca,' she said, 'you are up here all alone. Now you've got to get down by yourself!'

She had to concentrate very hard. Everything happened twice as fast as usual. Before she knew it she was already making the preparations for landing, watching for the moment to swing onto the final approach.

When she did, a new sense of confidence ran through her. Slowly the plane slipped through the sky, gradually losing height. 'Remember that picture,' she told herself. 'You're going down a slide; at the end you'll step off.'

Down and down she slid. She concentrated very hard. 'Not too soon,' she said out loud. 'Remember to hold off!'

Afterwards, she couldn't remember those last few moments. She must have been so focused, so concentrated on the job. All she knew was that, quite suddenly, she was down and the plane was running along the runway.

As she drove the plane back towards the hangar, a huge sense of achievement ran through her, greater than she'd ever felt before in her life. She had flown a plane solo; no one would be able to take that from her as long as she lived. A new smile began to spread across her face. This time she didn't stop it.

Tom came running towards her before she'd even brought the plane to a stop.

Chapter 13 *A declaration of war*

Francesca couldn't remember ever having been happier than she was that evening. When she got home, the first thing she did was make a Skype call to her family. Her mother's reaction made her laugh.

'Oh no, Francesca! Please don't say that!' her mother cried. 'Please don't tell me you've been up there all alone. Whatever was your stupid instructor thinking of!'

'But Mamma, you have to go solo some time!' Francesca answered.

'Well, why didn't he warn you? Why didn't he tell you beforehand?' Francesca's mother protested.

'Oh, Mamma, think about it!' Francesca replied. 'If your instructor warned you in advance, it would be disastrous. Can you imagine how nervous you'd get?'

'Well, please don't do it again, that's all,' her mother said.

'But of course I will, Mamma,' Francesca answered. 'That's the whole point!'

When Francesca finally returned downstairs, the Thompsons produced a bottle of champagne to celebrate. Francesca had an extraordinary sensation at that moment – as though she was walking on air. If someone had asked her, she half imagined she might be able to fly herself.

That evening Tom came round and took her out for a meal to celebrate. This time Francesca insisted on sharing the cost. The restaurant – Italian, of course – was beside the river, and they sat outside in the evening sunshine, overlooking the water. When the meal was finished, they went for a walk along the river bank until they came to a bench. They sat there for a time, chatting quietly, all the time watching a couple of white swans in the water in front of them, the birds circling elegantly in the water, as if admiring one another. Francesca couldn't think of a more perfect English setting. Sunshine sparkled on the water, setting a million diamonds dancing on the surface of the river.

When Tom drove her home, they sat in the car for a long time, with the engine running. At last, with her heart bursting with all the magic of the day, Francesca could stop herself no longer.

'Tom,' she said suddenly, 'you know, if you don't kiss me, I'm going to be very upset.'

Tom looked at her in astonishment. Then, very slowly, not quite believing his luck, he leant across and softly kissed her on the lips. They broke apart, looking at one another as if seeing each other properly for the first time, then kissed again. After a minute or two like this, Tom pulled away.

'I can't believe this is happening,' he said quietly.

Francesca looked at with him amusement. 'You'd better kiss me again in that case,' she said.

* * *

It was about ten o'clock the following morning when Francesca's mobile rang. Since she was expecting a call from Tom, she didn't even bother to glance at the screen.

'Hello,' she said happily.

'Why did you lie to me?' a man's voice asked roughly.

Francesca was so shocked, that for a second or two, she didn't realise who it was. Then she felt her stomach drop.

'I asked you why you lied to me,' Doug repeated even

more brutally. 'Why couldn't you find the courage to tell me what you were planning?'

Francesca was still too astonished to react sensibly. She suddenly felt a terrible sense of disappointment. Had everything that previous day been just a dream? All her happiness had been swept away in a flash.

'I asked you a question!' Doug was almost shouting.

'I don't know what you mean,' Francesca managed to say at last. 'I—'

Doug cut her short. 'Don't play that game with me,' he growled. 'Do you think I'm stupid? I know very well you've joined Flying Start. I heard you on the radio yesterday making your calls to the control tower. Did you really imagine I wouldn't find out? What was it – first solo?'

Doug sounded almost mad. Francesca still couldn't quite believe what she was hearing, but the man was just getting started.

'You tricked me!' he went on bitterly. 'You told me you were going back to Switzerland just so you could get your money back. And all the time you were planning to switch to that useless lot at Flying Start.'

'I wasn't!' Francesca broke in.

'I don't believe you,' Doug answered.

'It's true,' Francesca protested. 'I was going home. I only changed my mind because ...'

'Because what?' Doug said bitterly. 'I trust you're not going to give me any of that rubbish about touching you up.'

'It wasn't rubbish,' Francesca said, starting to fight back.

'Oh yes? Perhaps you'd like to prove it then,' Doug said, almost spitting out the words.

'But it's the truth!' Francesca responded. She was suddenly

filled with panic, thinking of that other woman's experience when she'd made accusations against Doug. 'You know it's the truth!' she went on more desperately. 'Right from the very first day you were making horrible remarks and asking me about my boyfriend, then trying to scare me so you could put your horrible hands all over me. Just because I'm young and foreign it doesn't mean you can do as you please. Did you really imagine that I might be interested in you? I think you're disgusting. If you were the last man on earth, I wouldn't look at you twice!' Doug didn't respond for a moment, then he burst out suddenly.

'How dare you!' he shouted. 'You're going to regret what you just said! Do you hear me?'

Francesca was shocked into silence.

'I said, "Do you hear me?"' Doug repeated.

Francesca didn't know what to say. Finally, it was all too much. A rush of Italian spilled from her mouth – words she didn't normally use – then she ended the call.

With that she collapsed down onto the chair beside her. For some time afterwards she stared at the phone, not believing what had just happened. Her heart was beating very fast and her hand was shaking. She couldn't seem to get her breath.

Then a dreadful feeling began to sweep over her. Something terrible had just taken place, something that couldn't be reversed. What had happened was like a declaration of war. From now on she wouldn't be able to relax for a minute. Doug was a madman. There was no telling what he might do next.

Chapter 14 *Learning a lesson*

Francesca didn't tell Tom – or anyone else, for that matter – about Doug's phone call. She didn't want to talk about it, or even think about it. In that way she could try and pretend it had never happened.

Nevertheless, when she arrived at the airfield for her next lesson on Thursday afternoon, Tom immediately spotted there was something wrong. Although she might have been able to disguise her voice on the phone, it was more difficult to hide it from her appearance. She'd hardly slept all night and she felt terrible.

He jumped up the moment she came into the office and hurried over to her.

'Are you OK?' he asked, looking concerned.

'Why, don't I look it?' Francesca answered sharply.

Tom seemed hurt. Frowning a little, he immediately said, 'You look absolutely great. I'm sorry, I just thought you seemed a bit worried when you came in, that's all.'

'I guess I'll have to do better then,' Francesca answered. Then, doubly ashamed for treating Tom so unfairly, she said. 'Sorry. I've just had a bad morning with the children. I didn't mean to be so horriblc.'

Tom look relieved. They kissed briefly, then Francesca looked around. 'Where's George?' she asked.

'He's on his way,' Tom answered. 'He phoned a short while ago to say he's stuck in traffic.' Tom paused. 'But I've just heard some interesting news,' he said.

'What's that?' Francesca asked.

Tom gave something of a strange look. 'Well, I've just been talking to a guy who keeps his aircraft in the same hangar as Doug's,' he said.

'Why? What's happened?' Francesca asked impatiently.

Tom raised his eyebrows. 'Well, according to this guy, Doug spent the night sleeping in the Fastwings office!'

'What!' Francesca said.

'That's what the guy said,' Tom went on. 'Apparently, when he came in this morning, he found Doug in a sleeping bag on the sofa in his office. It seems his wife has thrown him out and he's sleeping there until he can make other arrangements.'

Francesca was too shocked to speak for a moment. Sitting down, she tried to think it through. It certainly helped to explain the madness of the phone call she'd received from Doug. Perhaps he was having some kind of mental breakdown? But how would that affect her? Did it make things better or worse for her?

'I must say I've never liked Doug very much,' Tom went on, 'but I wouldn't wish a family break-up on anyone. You met his wife and kids, didn't you?'

'Yes,' Francesca answered distantly. Then, after a moment or two, she added, 'Do you know what it's all about?'

Tom shook his head. 'No, that's all Doug told this guy. I don't suppose it's the sort of thing you want to talk about very much.'

Francesca didn't comment. A picture had come into her mind: Doug having been thrown out of his home, sitting in his office, on his mobile phone to her, bitter and furious, striking out at anyone who had upset him. She had no idea where he was when he'd phoned her, of course, but the picture stuck in her mind. He seemed suddenly more dangerous, more unpredictable than ever.

She was just about to tell Tom about Doug's phone call, when George came in.

'You two look a bit suspicious,' he said. 'What's up?'

Tom retold the story. When he'd finished, George simply said, 'Sorry, I don't have much sympathy. From what I've heard he's a bit of a womaniser. No doubt his wife's had enough of him. He probably deserves all he gets.' He smiled at Francesca. 'Pleased you moved to us?'

Francesca nodded, at the same time wondering exactly what George meant about Doug being a womaniser. But there was no time to ask.

'Right, let's get flying,' George said. 'This afternoon you're going to fly me down to Beccles. There's a nice little grass airfield there where you can practise some more solo landings. How does that sound?'

Francesca found it difficult to concentrate at first when they climbed into the Cessna. Her mind was still focused on the news about Doug. Besides, as they approached the runway she kept thinking that he might have just picked up her call to the control tower and would know she was at the airfield now. She tried to tell herself that it made no difference, that there was nothing he could do. But she still felt very nervous.

It wasn't until they'd taken off that she began to relax.

'That's better,' George commented. 'I was beginning to think you were a different person from the girl who went solo last week.'

They flew on over farmland: large fields of corn, and grassy fields with cattle in. The cows looked tiny, like small beetles creeping across a green sheet. Every now and again a small wood, or the grounds of a big house, provided some contrast.

After about twenty minutes, a small group of hangars appeared under the nose of the aircraft, and then the broad line of a pale green runway cut through the grass. George announced their arrival over the radio and told Francesca to fly round to make their approach from the west. She did as instructed.

Beccles was a much smaller airfield than Norwich and the runway looked impossibly short.

'Just keep your eyes on the piano keys,' George told her. 'And use the throttle to control the height.'

They came in a bit too fast. The plane flew on far beyond the piano keys and landed with a heavy bump. But the aircraft quickly slowed to a stop on the grass runway. George told her to take the plane over to a small group of hangars.

When they'd stopped, George turned to her. 'Right, I'm going to have a cup of tea with my friend, Stan, in the office here. And while I'm doing that, I want you to do three landings. When you've finished, don't forget to come and pick me up.'

After George had climbed out and hurried off, Francesca tried to refocus her thoughts. She felt more worried this time, much more so than when George had sent her off on her first solo. She wondered whether he would have been happy for her to fly if he knew all the things that were occupying her mind. Perhaps she should have told him, confessed that she hadn't really slept.

Francesca went back to the start of the runway and a minute later she was speeding over the grass and pulling back gently on the control column, up in the air once more.

Almost immediately, as she began climbing to height, she felt her brain begin to clear. It was as if a screen in her head was being wiped clean; suddenly all her fears and concerns about Doug disappeared. There was only Francesca and her plane.

She flew round in a tight circle, glancing happily down at the hangars where she'd just left George, then concentrated on turning for the landing run.

With each landing, her technique improved and her confidence grew. After the third landing, she took the plane over to where George was already waiting on the grass.

'Well done,' he said simply, as he climbed into the plane. 'Now, take me home, please. It's beginning to get cold.'

What George had said was true: it was beginning to feel colder. The wind was picking up slightly and there was a chill in the air. Francesca shivered suddenly.

They took off and began climbing to height.

Then, when they'd reached about 500 feet, George slowly stretched forward and pulled out the throttle.

'You have engine failure,' he said.

For a moment or two Francesca didn't know what was happening. The power died instantly, and with it, all the speed. An unnatural silence filled the cabin. Francesca felt panic flood through her body. The next second the stall-warning alarm sounded.

At the last moment, just as George was about to take over, Francesca reacted. She pushed the control column forward and dropped the nose. Almost immediately, the stall-warning alarm fell silent, the speed picked up again and the frightening sense that they were about to drop out of the sky died. But still there was no power.

'Where are you going to land?' George asked calmly.

'The airfield?' Francesca replied.

'No,' George said firmly. 'Never try to turn back!'

Francesca searched the horizon ahead for an open field. Some way in front, beside some trees, there was a long green field. 'That one over there, then!' she shouted.

'Which one?' George asked.

'The one on the right!'

They continued slipping down. 350 feet, 300; all of a sudden they were down to 200.

At last George reached for the throttle. The power recovered at once and the speed picked up.

Francesca pulled back on the control column in relief, her blood flowing freely once again.

When they'd regained some height, George looked across at her. 'I thought you'd done an "engine-failure-on-take-off" when you were with Fastwings?'

'No,' Francesca answered.

George shook his head in disgust. 'That man Barker is worse than I thought. Well, let it be a lesson to you,' he went on, more seriously than she'd ever heard him before. 'An engine can fail at any time, especially during take-off. If it fails, you've got to act quickly. Drop the nose and look for somewhere to land. And keep up your speed. If you don't, we won't need to bury you – you'll make your own hole in the ground.'

Chapter 15   *Nowhere to hide*

The following week, at about ten o'clock in the morning, Francesca was returning to the house after taking the children to school.

She was nearly home when she noticed the grey Audi on the other side of Brabazon Road. It was just one of many other cars, but Francesca immediately thought of Doug's. His was a grey Audi, she was certain, but was it the same model? She felt her whole body tense up and tried not to look.

As she turned into the drive of the Thompsons' house, she couldn't stop herself glancing across at the car. Was there someone sitting in the driving seat? The sun was reflecting on the glass and it wasn't easy to see inside. She looked at the number plate. She only dared look for half a second, and she could only take in the first three letters.

With a horrible feeling growing in her throat, Francesca let herself into the house and hurried upstairs to her room. Keeping back in the shadow, she slowly approached the window and looked out. The car was still there, half-visible behind a tree, like a wolf hiding in the wood, a grey creature creeping about, ready to leap. She watched for at least a minute, unconsciously holding her breath. Then the car suddenly pulled away and raced off up the road.

For the rest of the day Francesca couldn't get the memory of the car out of her head. She couldn't be sure it was Doug's. On one hand, she knew very well that plenty of people drove grey Audis, but on the other hand it seemed too much of a coincidence that a car just like Doug's should be parked opposite her house. But if it was him, what on earth was he doing? The idea that he might be following her filled her with sudden terror. She felt sick as she remembered the day he had given her a lift home. Of course, he knew where she lived.

Francesca's anxiety grew all day. She tried to occupy her thoughts by keeping busy: cleaning the house with extra thoroughness and making a cake. But several times she went back to her bedroom window to see if the car had returned. And when she went to fetch the children from school, she couldn't get rid of the feeling that Doug might be there, hiding behind a tree, or creeping along behind her.

That evening Tom had invited Francesca for a meal at his flat. It was the first time she'd seen where he lived, and she could tell immediately that he'd gone to a lot of trouble in order to impress her. He'd obviously been busy tidying because everywhere smelt of cleaning products, and there were flowers and candles on the table.

The evening started well. The flat was full of Tom's drawings and paintings, and just as Francesca had guessed, they were brilliant – detailed drawings of birds like owls and hawks, aircraft painted against beautiful skies, and then a whole series of pencil drawings of a young girl, Tom's niece apparently. The expressions on the child's face were so real that Francesca thought the girl might suddenly come to life and step out of the picture.

'Have you ever tried to sell your work?' Francesca asked.

'I didn't think it was good enough,' Tom answered.

Francesca shook her head in astonishment. 'Tom, you must,' she said. Then she added more quietly, 'Would you do a drawing of me some time? I could send it to my family – they'd love it. I'll pay you, of course.'

'I'd love to,' Tom replied, delighted. 'But if you try and give me any money, I'll be very upset.'

Tom had made a great effort with the meal, too. For the first course, he'd made a tomato salad – using the very best 'buffalo' mozzarella cheese, and then for the main course, a mushroom risotto, which was delicious. Francesca could see Tom felt very proud that the meal had turned out so well, and she liked him even more for all the attention he gave. The more she got to know him, the more she felt that this was the sort of person he was – an artist – and he'd spent his whole life trying to be someone different. Perhaps his father was to blame, wanting Tom to be a copy of himself.

But despite all Tom's efforts, Francesca couldn't fully relax. She kept thinking about the grey Audi. Should she tell Tom about it or not? Would he think she was crazy? After the meal, Tom made some coffee and they went over to his sofa. Francesca knew that Tom was hoping that the evening would end romantically.

'I was just thinking,' she said, unable to stop herself at last. 'Do you know what kind of car Doug drives?'

Tom frowned in disappointment. 'An Audi, I think. Why?'

'No reason,' Francesca answered quickly. 'I just thought I might have seen his car in our road today, that's all.'

'But what would Doug be doing there?' Tom asked innocently.

'I don't know,' Francesca answered. 'That's why I wanted to check on his car. Do you know what the number plate is?'

Tom looked at her in confusion.

Francesca shook her head. 'No, of course you wouldn't. That was a bit of a stupid question.'

With that she changed the subject. Doing so made her even angrier with herself than she was already. She knew that she ought to tell Tom the true reason for her concern; this was the perfect moment to get the whole business out in the open. But for some reason she couldn't. The more time went on, the more difficult it was.

After a while, Francesca asked Tom to take her home, complaining of a headache. Francesca could see that it hurt him badly and was a blow to his confidence, but he was too much of gentleman to say anything.

Francesca was silent on the way home, full of anger with herself for spoiling the evening. If only she'd never begun lessons with Fastwings! If only she'd never met Doug!

Tom kissed her sweetly when he dropped her home, but Francesca ran inside before he could see the tears rolling down her cheeks. She couldn't believe what was happening to her. This was the second time she'd cried in less than a month.

* * *

The following Tuesday George sent Francesca off on her first 'landaway'.

'What's that?' Francesca asked.

'You go off on your own to land at another airfield, and then, with a bit of luck, you come back,' George replied cheerfully. 'I want you to fly down to Beccles just like we did last week. Go into the office, get Stan to sign your logbook, then fly straight back here. Sound simple enough?'

Francesca couldn't wait to get into the air. The last three days had been a nightmare of anxiety – checking the street for signs of Doug, trying to decide what to do. When she'd arrived at the airfield earlier, she'd resisted the temptation to go straight to look for Doug's car and check the number plate. She would try to do it after her lesson, but now she needed to concentrate on flying. Soon, she thought, she would be up in the air and all those fears would melt away.

But as she approached the runway, she felt as tense as ever. Was Doug at the airfield now? Was he listening in to the radio calls? Did he know she was there?

Once she'd taken off, however, as if by magic, her anxiety began to slip away. She climbed steadily to 3000 feet, then turned south-east and headed for Beccles. It was a beautiful day, the colours of the sky and fields below intensely clear and bright. Looking down the length of the wings, she had the sensation once more that they might be her arms. She moved the control column left and right very gently and watched with delight how the wings responded. It gave her a huge sense of freedom. She was untouchable up there in the sky, completely out of reach!

The landing at Beccles went well, and Stan was friendly when she went to get her logbook signed. She loved the little airfield with its grass runway and handful of light aircraft. It made her feel connected to all the aviators of the past, taking to the skies in wooden aircraft and open cockpits.

Refusing a cup of tea and saying she ought to head home, Francesca climbed back into the plane and very soon took off. As she turned towards Norwich, she radioed back to Stan below and said a cheerful goodbye.

It was about five minutes later, when she'd reached 3000 feet, that an odd sensation came to her. Performing her regular check of the sky around, she caught sight of something over her shoulder. Immediately, she looked behind. A plane – another Cessna – was flying very close to her, perhaps ten metres below and as many metres behind.

The shock almost made her let go of the control column. It was Doug in the Fastwings Cessna. She glanced behind again and saw him quite clearly; he was looking out of the cockpit window and staring directly at her.

Francesca wanted to scream. A terrible panic rushed up through her body, paralysing her for a minute. Suddenly, she didn't know how to fly the plane, or what any of the controls were for. She didn't want to look round, and yet she couldn't stop herself. But every time she did, Doug was still there, his sunglasses staring blindly back.

She felt helpless, with no idea what to do. All of a sudden she realised he must have followed her to Beccles, then circled somewhere overhead until he heard her make her take-off calls. Then he'd come swooping down out of the sky, just like a hawk. But what did he want? Was he just trying to scare her or would he try to make her crash? She flew on, her hands shaking on the control column, trying to imagine what would happen next.

And then, just as suddenly as he'd appeared on her shoulder, he was gone. The next time she looked round, there was no sign of the aircraft anywhere. She searched the sky, but the plane had simply disappeared.

When she finally landed back at Norwich, George and Tom were both waiting for her.

'How was it then?' Tom asked.

'Fine. Just fine,' Francesca answered weakly.

'You look a bit pale,' he went on anxiously. 'Do you feel all right?'

Francesca didn't say anything. Without another word, she hurried through to the toilets at the back of the hangar and was violently sick.

Chapter 16   *The stalker*

Francesca was watching television that evening, when she heard a text arrive on her phone. Thinking it would be Tom, she immediately opened the message.

'Sorry if I frightened you!' she read. *'For a moment I was afraid you might crash! Best of luck with the rest of your lessons. Doug'*

Francesca didn't know what to do with herself for the rest of the evening. She wanted to scream out loud. The man was hunting her, following her around, keeping at a safe distance, but making sure she knew he was there all the time. There was a word for what he was doing – the man was stalking her; he was a stalker. It was the same word in Italian.

She felt a great knot of anger growing in her chest. What did he want? Somehow it seemed to her that Doug was no longer interested in her for sex, it was as though things had gone beyond that desire. Now what he wanted was to make her suffer as much as he could. Wasn't that the point of the message? 'Sorry if I frightened you' meant just the opposite. He wasn't wishing her good luck with her lessons. Doug was determined to scare her to death.

Lying in bed that night, Francesca tried to decide what she could do. The idea of going to the police was out of the question. What would she tell them? That the man had put his hand on her knee and touched her a couple of times? What else had he done? He didn't even have her money any more. There had been a couple of angry phone calls, she 'thought' she'd seen his car outside the house, and now he'd flown up alongside her. Even the text message could be read as nothing more than cheerful good wishes. The police would laugh at her, and yet she *knew* Doug was stalking her.

So, what about telling someone else: for instance, telling Tom or Mrs Thompson what was going on? How would that help? What could they do? What if she told Tom the whole story? How would he react? She knew he'd do everything he could – she could picture him bravely marching up to the Fastwings hangar and getting into a fight with Doug. Although she liked the idea of a courageous Tom coming to her rescue, it wasn't something she could ever accept. Francesca always fought her own battles and she didn't let others take her place. By the time she finally fell asleep, Francesca had decided that if she was going to stay in England, the only thing to do was to go and see Doug herself.

* * *

The next morning, once she'd taken the children to school, Francesca took the bus straight up to the airfield. She didn't tell Tom she was coming – indeed, she didn't even call in at the Flying Start office. Instead she went straight to Fastwings.

Outside the entrance, she paused for a moment or two and tried to calm her nerves. Then, before she could change her mind, she went directly inside and down the small corridor to the Fastwings office.

As soon as she reached it, she could see through the glass door that Doug wasn't there. A strange sense of anti-climax ran through her. Having prepared herself so bravely for meeting up with him, it seemed doubly cruel that it should all be for nothing.

She didn't know what to do. She couldn't wait long: she had jobs to do at home for Mrs Thompson that morning.

She was still trying to decide how long to wait, when a strange feeling made her turn round. Doug was standing there, only a couple of metres behind her. He was holding a large hammer. Francesca felt very frightened.

'Well, well, this is a surprise,' Doug said, with a look of slight amusement. Then, seeing Francesca's expression, he gave a small wave with the hammer. 'It's all right, just a problem with the hangar door. Nothing for you to worry about,' he said. 'Just yet …' he added, giving a short laugh.

Francesca tried not to lose her nerve. 'I'd like to talk to you for a minute,' she said.

'Of course, come into the office. Is it just you or have you got your lawyer with you?' he asked with heavy sarcasm.

Francesca ignored the remark. She didn't want to go inside, but there seemed little choice. Swallowing hard, she followed Doug through into the office. As she did so, she caught a faint smell of alcohol in the atmosphere. Had he been drinking? The thought frightened her even more. He dropped the hammer on his desk and gestured to her to sit down. Francesca wanted to remain standing, but Doug was already sitting behind his desk with his feet on the table. She sat on the edge of the sofa opposite, trying not to look directly at him. There was a weird look in his eyes.

'So, have you got fed up with Flying Start?' Doug asked with a curling lip. 'Or has lover boy tried to push his luck too far?' he added, then smiled with satisfaction at Francesca's shock.

Francesca was taken completely off guard. How had he found out about her and Tom? Had someone told him?

'Oh yes,' Doug went on, 'I know all about you and Tom Brennan. You should find somewhere more private, Francesca. Really – climbing all over one another in his Ford Focus! I thought you'd have more style than that. And with a loser like him! Honestly, Francesca!' He grinned once again. 'Anyway, I didn't mean to spoil your visit with cheap insults about your boyfriend. Perhaps you've come to apologise?'

Francesca felt sick for a moment. When she'd decided to come and see Doug, she'd imagined the meeting quite differently. She'd imagined marching into his office and making her speech confidently, without fear, in a sensible adult manner. But Doug had caught her by surprise. He must have been in Brabazon Road one night when Tom had taken her home. He must have been spying on them for ages. The idea filled her with fresh anger.

'Me? Apologise! I shall never apologise to you,' she began, trying to keep control of her voice. 'I came to tell you to leave me alone.'

Doug gave a small frown. 'I'm sorry, Francesca,' he said, 'I don't think I quite understand.'

Francesca closed her eyes. How had it come to this? Did she really deserve this misery? All she wanted was to learn to fly. 'You're stalking me,' she said quietly. 'I know you are. You've been following me in your car; now you're following me in your plane.'

Doug gave a look of astonishment. It was pure acting, Francesca knew it was. Even Doug seemed to know it wasn't convincing.

Pushing back against his chair, he put his hands together behind his head.

'I'm sorry, Francesca, but I can't believe what I'm hearing,' he said. 'Are you really accusing me of *stalking* you, just because I happened to be flying over Beccles at the same time as you a couple of days ago? Do we men have to keep out of the air every time Francesca Bartolli takes to the skies?'

Francesca tried to keep herself calm. 'But you were! You were stalking me!' she exclaimed. 'I've seen your car outside my house in Brabazon Road and you've just admitted seeing Tom and me in his car! You're following me around and spying on me! Why are you doing this? What do you want from me?'

Doug watched Francesca for a little while, all the time the same cruel smile playing at his lips. Then, with the amusement dying on his face, he slowly took his feet from the desk and sat forward with a cold bitter expression.

'I don't want anything from you, Francesca,' he said. 'OK, it might have been nice if you'd been more … how shall I put it … friendly? Indeed, I might have reduced your flying fees even more if you had!' He gave a strange laugh at the idea for a moment, and Francesca wondered again if he'd been drinking. Then he immediately grew serious again. 'But that time has long gone, my dear. Now I get a kick from just seeing the terror on your face.'

He paused, watching Francesca with cold lifeless eyes. Francesca was reminded of a snake.

'So you admit that you've been stalking me!' she said desperately.

Doug continued staring at her. 'I admit nothing. If you think I've been stalking you, then prove it,' he said, his voice getting louder. 'Now, get out of my office before I call the police. I haven't got time for this!'

As he said that, Doug picked up the hammer he had left on the desk and smashed it down as hard as possible on the wood. There was a tremendous crash and part of the desk cracked, sending a tray spinning to the floor.

'Didn't you hear me!' Doug shouted, his eyes wild with madness. 'I told you to get out! Don't you understand the English language?'

Francesca froze. The man was completely out of control. He *was* drunk. She rushed for the door. As she left the office, she looked back to see Doug getting up from his chair, the hammer still gripped tightly in his hand.

She ran down the corridor and out into the open air in genuine fear of her life. She didn't stop shaking until she was safely on the bus home. There, as she sat hiding her face in her hands, a little old lady asked her if she was feeling all right.

'Yes, I think so,' Francesca answered. Then, realising it was a bit of an odd reply, she added, 'I nearly got myself killed a minute ago – when I was crossing the road.'

Chapter 17 *A matter of practice*

For the next four days, apart from taking the children to and from school, Francesca didn't leave the house. She simply didn't feel safe. Saying she had a bad headache, she even cancelled her next flying lesson on Thursday afternoon. At the weekend Tom invited her out twice, but she refused both times. She sat miserably in her room, unable to concentrate on anything and trying not to go to the window to look out.

By Monday morning she'd almost made a final decision to go back to Switzerland – one hundred percent definitely this time. How her relationship with Tom could survive after that she couldn't imagine. Whatever the case, she decided to ring Flying Start that morning and cancel her lesson the next day.

Listening to the number ring, she half hoped somebody other than Tom would answer, but of course it was him.

'Hello,' he said brightly. 'Flying Start.'

'Tom,' she said quietly, 'it's Francesca. Tom,' she went on before he could say anything, 'I'm just ringing to say I still don't think I'm well enough for tomorrow's lesson.'

Tom's voice dropped immediately. 'Oh no, poor you! Really? Is your headache still bad?'

Francesca felt like a complete fraud. She knew she had to talk to him. She was about to say something when Tom interrupted.

'I was so much hoping you'd be OK – and I heard a bit of news this morning that I thought would interest you.'

'What?' Francesca asked.

'Fastwings has gone out of business,' Tom said.

Francesca wasn't sure she understood. 'What do you mean?' she asked.

'I mean Doug's finished, that's what I mean,' Tom replied. 'Apparently there's a notice on his office door this morning saying "Fastwings regrets to announce that, with immediate effect, it has stopped trading". What's more, I've heard his Cessna is up for sale on the Internet.'

Tom finally came to the end of his speech. All the while he'd been speaking Francesca had been trying to absorb the news and what it meant for her. Did it mean there was a chance she would be able to continue with her flying lessons? Did it mean she could stay in England after all?

'Francesca? Are you still there?' Tom asked.

'Yes ... yes, of course,' Francesca answered. 'But I was just thinking ... I suppose that means Doug won't be up at the airfield any more ...'

'I can't see why he should be,' Tom replied. 'Anyway, apparently he's left Norwich and run off up north. But you won't be sorry about that, will you?'

'No, no I won't,' Francesca answered. It seemed to her as if ice was melting around her. For days her body had felt frozen. Now the sun had come out again; there was life!

'Anyway,' Tom went on, 'Thank God you got out in time. I mean, if you were still having lessons with him, you might have lost all your money.'

'Really?' Francesca said.

'Yes, sure. You could have lost the lot!' Tom continued. 'Come to think of it, I guess losing your business can't have helped him much.'

'Yes,' Francesca answered. She'd been thinking the same herself; perhaps that was why he seemed to hate her so much.

'Anyway,' Tom said, breaking into her thoughts. 'Are you sure you won't be well enough for the lesson tomorrow?'

'What do you mean?' she asked.

'Your headache,' Tom said, sounding a little confused.

'Oh, that,' Francesca answered, even more ashamed now about her excuse. 'On second thoughts, perhaps it would do it good if I got out for a while.'

'Brilliant,' Tom said. 'In that case, is there any chance I could see you tonight?'

Francesca felt a smile breaking out on her face. 'All right, I don't see why not,' she said happily. 'That would be great.'

*   *   *

The next afternoon, Francesca was 3000 feet above the East Anglian fields, flying with George again. They'd been practising advanced turns, first putting the aircraft into a tight 45-degree turn, and then even tighter, so that the plane was over on its side at 60 degrees or more. Francesca's head was spinning. Pulling back on the control column and holding the nose level on the horizon had made her feel quite dizzy.

Francesca was feeling a little dizzy too with everything that was happening in the rest of her life. Knowing that Doug wasn't in Norwich any more, meant life could return to normal. She was still afraid though that it might all be a dream and she would turn a corner and find the grey Audi waiting there. But no one had seen any sign of Doug at the airfield and she began to believe it at last.

And then there was Tom. In the few days since his phone call, things had become much more serious in their relationship. Perhaps the thought of returning to Switzerland and breaking up with him had concentrated her mind. Whatever it was, Francesca had come to see very clearly that she wasn't just fond of Tom. She was most definitely in love.

'I think it's about time we did a PFL,' George said, interrupting her thoughts.

'What's that?' Francesca asked.

'A PFL?' George replied. 'A PFL is a practice forced landing – a bit like we did last time – engine failure, but this time from higher up. I pull out the throttle, you choose a field in which to land, then we can glide down doing all the engine checks and emergency calls.'

'And do we actually land?' Francesca asked.

'Not unless you want to pay the farmer for damage to his field,' George said, smiling. 'But we do go down to about 200 feet – low enough to see if we'd survive the landing.'

'Sounds fun,' Francesca answered, who was growing in confidence with each flying-hour that passed.

They flew on for a couple of minutes, then George reached forward slowly and pulled out the throttle. Instantly, the engine noise died and Francesca felt the plane slow.

'You have engine failure, Ms Bartolli,' George said quietly.

This time Francesca reacted quickly. Pushing the control column forward, she put the aircraft into a gentle glide and felt the speed pick up again.

'Good,' George said calmly. 'Now, where are you going to land?'

Francesca looked down to the ground far below. There was a wood away to the left, then, nearer to the plane, a series of fields. The biggest was a large brown one, just below the nose.

'That one,' Francesca replied, pointing with her free hand.

'Mmm, I find ploughed fields a bit bumpy to land on,' George said quietly. 'Don't you think a grassy one would be better?'

Francesca immediately felt foolish. Brown meant ploughed; green meant grass. She couldn't believe she had made such a basic mistake.

'Come on, make a decision quickly,' George said cheerfully. 'You've already lost 300 feet in height.'

Francesca looked down in desperation. Almost directly below there was a long thin green field.

'That one, then!' she said, pointing again.

George glanced down. 'Your decision,' he said. 'Now, you need to land into the wind. Which way is the wind blowing?'

Francesca panicked. 'I can't remember,' she said.

'Well, look for some smoke!' George called.

Francesca searched the sky. Far away to the right she spotted the chimney of a factory. The smoke was blowing towards them. That meant, to land in the field below, Francesca had to fly round in a circle. Still disturbed by her mistake, she began to turn.

'2300 feet,' George said. 'Right, don't forget your emergency calls!'

Francesca's mind went blank. She couldn't remember a word of what she'd learnt. The panicky feeling in her chest got worse. The plane was sinking fast.

'I can't remember,' she said.

George reminded her. 'Mayday, mayday, mayday,' he said. 'And don't forget this is only a practice, so don't press the radio button!'

Francesca swallowed hard. 'Mayday! Mayday! Mayday!' she called, then came to a stop. What was she meant to say next? She remembered she had to say the details of the plane and half a dozen other things, but everything became confused in her head. 'Sorry,' she said, hopelessly.

'All right, forget the calls,' George said, trying to calm her. 'It's more important to land the plane safely. You're down to 1500 feet. You'll have to do a tight turn or you won't make it to the field.'

Francesca tried to concentrate, but now everything seemed to be going wrong. Unconsciously, she'd been pulling back on the control column, so the plane was flying dangerously slowly.

All of a sudden the stall-warning alarm sounded. Francesca froze.

This time, George didn't wait. 'All right, I have control,' he said. At once he reached for his control column and pushed it forward, at the same time increasing the power.

The plane picked up speed immediately and after a few moments George took it into a steady climb.

Francesca felt herself going red. 'I'm sorry,' she said. 'That was terrible, wasn't it?'

George gave a tiny nod of the head. 'Don't worry,' he said. 'Everyone makes a mess of it the first time.' Then he looked across and smiled. 'Besides, in forty years of flying I haven't had an engine failure once.'

Chapter 18 *Tempting fate*

Whenever Francesca either saw Tom or telephoned him over the next couple of weeks, she couldn't resist the temptation of asking if there was any news of Doug. There was none. No one seemed to have any idea where he was. A rumour went round the airfield that he'd gone abroad, but no one could confirm it. Whatever the case, the door to the Fastwings office remained firmly shut and there was no sign of his grey Audi.

Then, one evening when Francesca was at Tom's flat, he announced that he had some further news.

'I heard something else about Doug this morning, but I'm not sure you'll want to know,' he said.

Francesca felt herself tense up immediately. 'You'd better tell me,' she said quietly.

'Well,' Tom went on a little anxiously, 'it seems that before he came here, when he was an instructor down at Southampton, he was accused of sexually harassing one of his female students. The woman brought charges against him, but the case was dropped because she didn't have any proof and Doug won damages. But I can't believe a woman would go to the lengths of bringing charges against someone unless there was some truth in it. And I think you said you always felt very uncomfortable with him – I just thought that might explain why.'

Francesca had remained silent throughout Tom's speech and she didn't say anything now. She just didn't want to think about Doug.

'Sorry, perhaps it was a mistake to tell you,' Tom said, confused.

'No, it's all right,' she said at last. 'But I knew the story already.'

Tom looked very surprised. 'You knew it?' he said.

Francesca gave a sigh. She didn't understand why she was still so unwilling to talk about it, but she was.

With difficulty, she began, 'About a month ago, I searched for Doug on the Internet and I found a newspaper report about him. It's one of the reasons why I decided to leave Fastwings.'

'I'm not surprised,' Tom said quickly. 'I hope he didn't try anything like that with you.'

Francesca bit her lip. 'Well, actually, he did,' she said. 'That's the other reason I had to leave.'

'What?!' Tom cried.

Francesca felt sick again. 'He used to keep putting his hand on my leg and touching me,' she said. 'It was horrible – and he kept saying things, making sort of sexual suggestions. It was disgusting …'

Just as Francesca had guessed, Tom was furious and over the next five minutes Francesca was forced to relate all that had happened in the flying lessons. The memory of it all only brought Francesca's misery back, and, on the point of tears, she said she wanted to think about something else.

At least Tom had the sensitivity not to press her any further. Saying how sorry he was, and all the things he would do if he ever saw Doug again, he finished with a shake of his head.

'What I don't understand is how he ever got an instructor's licence,' he said.

'Yes,' Francesca murmured.

'Well, at least it's all over and you're safe now.'

Francesca didn't say anything. For some reason, she hadn't been able to bring herself to tell Tom about any of Doug's threats.

*   *   *

Francesca's next few lessons were much more successful. She managed some difficult crosswind landings very well and her confidence returned. So the lesson after that George made her try another PFL.

This time Francesca was much more focused, choosing a landing field quickly, noting the direction of the wind and turning the plane well. The emergency calls didn't go so well, but more importantly, as they glided down, it soon became clear that the field Francesca had selected was not a good choice. A telephone line stretched from one side of the field to the other. If she'd attempted to land she would have hit the wire for certain, and probably buried the plane deep in the earth.

Nevertheless, when they'd returned to Norwich and were back in the Flying Start office, George announced that the following Tuesday he wanted Francesca to do her 'cross-country flight'.

'What does that mean?' Francesca asked.

'It means you fly solo, landing at two different airfields before you return here.' George grinned. 'This is the last big flight before you do your final flying exam.'

*   *   *

Francesca couldn't believe how much planning was involved in such a flight. George had told her she was to fly to Leicester, then Peterborough and finally back to Norwich.

So she examined maps, learning the route and areas to be avoided, then studied information about the airfields. There were other things to consider, too: the fuel she needed to take, the radio calls she'd have to make. When she went to bed the night before the flight, her brain was full of a million facts and figures all competing for a place in her head.

Francesca woke on the Tuesday morning with an uncomfortable feeling. It was a curious sensation: nothing precise, just the sort of feeling that a bad dream sometimes leaves, a sort of shadow cast over the day.

She got up and pulled open the curtains, determined to forget the feeling. The weather was quite windy, but bright and clear, which meant good visibility. That was a relief: nothing would have been worse than discovering the flight was off.

Mrs Thompson had given her the whole day off and Tom had promised to come and pick her up, so at ten-thirty, Francesca was waiting at her window, ready to leave.

It was then that she saw the grey Audi. It crept slowly past the entrance to the drive, disappeared, then reappeared on the other side of the road half a minute later and stopped.

Francesca's heart sank. Doug was back. She was certain of it. She drew back from the window and collapsed onto the bed. Her hands tore at her hair in misery. 'Why! Why! Why!' she thought, 'Why can't he leave me alone!' She sat there, trying to fight her fears, trying to fight against the feeling that her heart was going to explode. Then the next moment, full of anger, she jumped up, determined to settle matters with the man once and for all.

She raced down the stairs, pulled open the front door angrily, and marched out into the drive.

But the Audi was no longer there. It had disappeared completely.

A couple of seconds later, Tom's car pulled into the drive and stopped.

'Today's the day!' he said cheerfully, climbing out of the driver's door. Then, seeing Francesca's face, he asked, 'Hey, are you all right?'

Francesca stood still on the spot. A sentence about Doug being back formed in her mouth, but wouldn't come out. Somehow, it seemed as long as she didn't say it, it wouldn't be true.

'Fine,' she answered quietly.

On the way to the airfield, her spirits began to rise. Perhaps she'd got it wrong after all. She couldn't actually be certain it *was* Doug's car – maybe it was someone else's car. Just a simple mistake. She rested her head back and tried to relax.

George was already waiting in the office when they arrived. He gave a slight frown as Francesca walked in.

'Everything all right?' he asked, looking at her closely.

'Of course,' Francesca answered.

George didn't seem convinced. 'Sure?' he asked.

'Well, a bit nervous, I guess,' Francesca said.

George nodded, apparently satisfied with the response. 'Well, that'll keep you focused,' he said. 'Right, I've printed out the weather report for you, so Tom and I will leave you to get down to the final planning now.'

Francesca tried to settle at the desk. She stared at the weather report George had given her, but none of the lines and numbers printed there meant anything to her. All she could see was Doug's car, creeping along the road.

The panicky feeling rose in her chest again as she tried to get the picture out of her head. Today of all days, she told herself, she really couldn't afford to have anything else in her mind except the cross-country flight. It would need all of her concentration – not simply flying the plane, but all the other tasks, too.

Fifteen minutes later, George came back.

'How's it going?' he asked.

Francesca showed him her flight plan – all the rows of figures she'd prepared. George studied it for a short time, then looked at her.

'Not bad,' he said. 'Except for one small point. Which way is the wind blowing today?'

'West to east,' Francesca replied.

'You've calculated everything east to west. Following this flight plan, you'd end up in the middle of the North Sea.'

He gave her a friendly smile and left. Francesca buried her head in her hands.

Twenty minutes later, after Francesca had corrected her error, and George had approved the plan, they left the office. The Flying Start Cessna was already outside the hangar, its blue and white paintwork shining brightly in the sun. Tom was cleaning the windscreen.

Francesca walked around the plane, looking over the body, the tyres and the lights, doing an oil-check. The fuel didn't need checking for water since the plane had already been flown that morning, but it needed filling up. She and Tom dragged the aircraft over to the fuel tank.

'For the flight you're doing, you'll need it filled right up to maximum,' Tom said. 'If you operate the pump, I'll take the fuel-line.'

'It's OK, I'll do it,' Francesca said. Taking the end of the fuel-line, she climbed up onto the wing, and opened the fuel-cap. Soon, with Tom at the pump, fuel was pouring into the tank. When it was full, Francesca took the line and climbed up onto the other wing.

'Stop,' she called, when the fuel reached the maximum point.

Tom gave a small frown. 'That's funny,' he said.

'Why?' Francesca asked.

'I thought she'd take a couple more litres than that.' He thought for a minute. 'Oh well, I suppose I must have noted down the wrong figures after the last flight yesterday. Not to worry.'

Francesca double-checked the levels, then climbed down.

'Right. Are you all ready?' Tom said cheerfully.

'I think so,' Francesca answered.

'Good luck, then,' Tom replied. He leant across and gave Francesca a brief kiss on the cheek. 'See you in about five hours' time,' he whispered in her ear.

Francesca didn't say anything. For some reason it felt too much like tempting fate.

Chapter 19 *One chance!*

Francesca climbed into the cockpit, settled into the seat and did up her safety harness. Then she arranged the flight plan on her knee and put the map on the other seat. Satisfied with all that, she called to Tom to stand clear, and started the engine. When that was running smoothly, she put on the headphones and tuned in the radio to Norwich Control Tower.

'Norwich Tower, this is Golf Lima Yankee,' she called.

The tower called back. Francesca announced that she was going to go round to the runway, then she released the brakes and the aircraft began to move forward. Tom gave her a firm thumbs-up sign, and watched as she began to move away.

As she went round past the hangars, Francesca's confidence began to grow again. Even if it was Doug she'd seen that morning, she was safe now – he couldn't reach her. With the Fastwings Cessna out of action, locked away in the hangar, he couldn't come swooping out of the sky as he had done previously. She could forget about Doug.

Focusing her mind on the flight ahead, she stopped before the start of the runway, and began the power checks. First she ran the engine up to full power, then let it drop back to almost nothing, making sure that it didn't cut out. Happy with that, she checked all the controls, moving the control column around, noting that there was full and free movement. Then she made the next radio call. 'Norwich Tower, Golf Lima Yankee is ready to line up runway zero nine.'

'Golf Lima Yankee,' the call came back, 'You are cleared for take-off runway zero nine.'

Francesca felt her heart beating faster. She released the brakes and, using the throttle carefully, powered the small aircraft onto the piano keys at the start of the runway. Then she waited there for a moment. This was the critical time. When she pushed in the throttle she would begin the take-off run, and then would come the point of no return. If she was going to change her mind, it had to be now.

She hesitated for perhaps three seconds, then actually spoke out loud in English, 'Come on! Don't be such a coward!'

The next moment she'd pushed in the throttle and already the little Cessna had started moving. The speed picked up fast. Francesca's eyes moved quickly between the dials and the runway ahead. A faint smile spread across her face, then before she realised she'd made the decision, she had already pulled back on the control column and the plane was in the air.

Holding the nose down, she put the aircraft into a climb. Soon the first five hundred feet were passed, and the airfield was left behind. She was out over fields, climbing steadily towards the clouds high up above. And as she flew, she began to feel that familiar sense of release – that sensation she had whenever she was in the air now. It was one of complete freedom, a kind of divorce from ordinary life, a belief that she was part of a completely different world from that of the Earth.

At 1000 feet, she began to turn the plane until she was flying in the correct direction towards Leicester. Looking down, she checked for the things she should see: a railway line entering a large wood. It was there. She was exactly on course.

She wasn't even a minute into the flight when the radio call came.

'Golf Lima Yankee. This is Norwich Tower.'

'Golf Lima Yankee,' she called back.

'Golf Lima Yankee. Return to Norwich immediately!'

Francesca couldn't believe her ears. Forgetting her radio language she asked, 'What was that?'

The call was returned instantly. 'Golf Lima Yankee, you must return to the airfield immediately. We have been informed that there is water in your fuel and you are in serious danger of engine failure!'

Francesca felt her blood run cold. 'Pardon?' she said faintly.

'Golf Lima Yankee, you are in danger of engine failure. Return to Norwich immediately. Do you understand?'

Weakly, Francesca answered. 'Yes, I understand.' With staring eyes, she began to turn the plane round. A hand seemed to be gripping her throat. She could hardly breathe. Of course, it was Doug. He had somehow put water in the fuel tank. If it reached the engine, the engine was certain to stop.

Another call came through. 'Golf Lima Yankee, please state your height and position.'

Francesca stared at the map, at the dials, down at the ground. For a moment, she was in total confusion. Then she called back.

'Norwich Tower,' she said slowly. 'Golf Lima Yankee is at 3000 feet, overhead Branton Wood, heading zero eight zero.'

'Very good, Golf Lima Yankee,' the tower answered. 'Emergency Services are standing by at Norwich. You have priority for landing.'

Francesca had no time to take in what had happened, for almost at the same moment, the engine coughed like an old man, went back to full power for a second or two, then stopped completely.

Francesca froze. She couldn't move, she couldn't speak.

Then it hit her. This was real. She had to act.

She blinked a couple of times as if suddenly waking up, then a new Francesca seemed to slip into the seat. Immediately she pushed the control column forward and put the plane into a glide. And then she was looking down through the left-hand window to the earth beneath. Fortunately, she had just left the woodland behind and there was a choice of fields below. A large green rectangular one caught her eye, but a thin wavy line through the middle of it suggested a small stream. A little way ahead, Francesca spotted another field, paler green this time – it would have to be that one.

She tried to work out which way she would land. She'd taken off to the west, now she was flying back in the opposite direction, so she must be flying east. If she was going to land into the wind, it meant turning 180 degrees. She would have to make a wide circle round, but make sure she didn't come in short. If she did, there were trees and a ploughed field – she would crash into these.

'Norwich Tower. Mayday! Mayday! Mayday! Golf Lima Yankee has engine failure,' she called. 'Attempting forced landing just east of Branton Wood.'

'Golf Lima Yankee,' the call came back, 'Emergency call

understood. Forced landing east of Branton Wood. Good luck.'

Francesca didn't answer. Already the plane was down to 1500 feet. She was over the middle of the field she had chosen – now she had to fly on and circle round to come into land.

Another cough from the engine caught her by surprise. Somehow, it must have restarted. Maybe she would be able to fly on, after all; perhaps there was hope! But as suddenly as the engine had restarted, it stopped again. Francesca swore. It would have been better if it hadn't restarted at all.

She had to concentrate. Concentrate like never before. 1000 feet. She should begin the turn. There were trees beneath, and a road. She could see a small white car racing along. Francesca imagined the driver happily speeding on, completely unaware of the drama taking place overhead.

Now five hundred feet. So, turn towards the field now. Keep up speed. Oh, God, Francesca thought, I'll never make it, it's too far ahead. She dropped the nose. The ground was getting closer with every second. And the trees. Unconsciously her hand went to the throttle to get more power, before she remembered there was no power, the engine had failed. 'Stupid!' she shouted out loud.

She looked ahead, down the nose. The field was approaching.

There was nothing for it. This was it. One chance to land. One chance to live!

'Here we go! Come on, Francesca!' she said. She thought of her family: of her mother and father and sister, and Tom. This is for you, she thought.

All of a sudden the ground was rushing past. The pale green suddenly formed into a line of balls; she pulled back on the control column.

The plane hung in the air for a moment or two, then dropped. With a heavy bump, it came down to the ground, all three wheels hitting the earth at the same time. Just before it stopped, the plane suddenly dug into the earth and dropped forward onto its nose.

Francesca was thrown tight against the safety harness, then back against the seat.

It took her four or five seconds to realise she wasn't moving any more. She looked around, unable to understand what she was seeing. Then she realised that lettuces were pressed up all around the window. She had landed in a lettuce field.

Through her headphones, she heard a call.

'Golf Lima Yankee?'

'Norwich Tower, this is Golf Lima Yankee,' she said. 'I am safely down on the ground.'

The next moment she burst into tears of relief.

Chapter 20   *A final test*

Three hours later, having left the Cessna in the temporary care of a very surprised farmer, Francesca was taken by police back to the airfield at Norwich.

'So, you're telling me Doug put water in my fuel and then he was the one who telephoned the control tower?' Francesca said.

She was back in the Flying Start office with Tom and George, gripping a cup of coffee tightly.

'Yes,' Tom answered miserably. 'I should have known there was something up when we couldn't get those other two litres of fuel in the tank. I don't know what to say Francesca; it's my fault.'

'Rubbish,' George broke in. 'There's only one person to blame, and it's not you. Just get on with the story.'

Tom hesitated for a moment, then continued.

'Well, it seems Doug was sitting in his car up here at the airfield, when he saw you going past, and suddenly he realised the seriousness of what he'd done. He claims he never imagined you'd even get as far as the runway – that the engine would cut out long before take-off and he just wanted to scare you. But when you went past it was like waking from a dream; he realised you might actually die and that he would be responsible for murder. Apparently, he called the control tower from his mobile just as you were taking off.'

Francesca shook her head in disbelief, and gripped her cup of coffee even tighter.

'And then he gave himself up to the police,' she said quietly.

'Yes,' Tom replied. 'Once he'd called the control tower, he phoned the police himself and just sat in his car until they arrived. He made no attempt to get away.'

Francesca shivered. 'The poor guy,' she said quietly. 'He really must be ill.'

'Insane, more like it,' George broke in. 'They should lock him up and throw away the key.'

Francesca smiled, touched by the anger that her instructor was showing. George reminded her of her grandfather, who, although the kindest and gentlest of men, would be furious at any mistreatment of a family member. She tried to change the subject.

'So, why didn't the engine stop immediately?'

'Ah,' said George, 'that's the remarkable thing.' He sat up. 'The point is this: at some time today after its first flight, the stupid fool got to the aircraft and poured a couple of litres of water into one of the tanks. Now, as you know, fuel floats on water, so with the tank up on the wing, the water would feed very quickly into the engine. However, there would have already been some fuel in the system, so clearly in driving round and taking off, you used up that fuel, and only a minute later the water got in. Then, the engine stopped!'

Francesca half understood. If she was totally honest, she wasn't fully listening. Every now and then, the true horror of what had happened hit her again. She'd been closer to death than at any time before in her life – at that moment, she might be lying dead in a field inside a broken plane. She shivered once again.

'I just hope the bloody fool hasn't put you off flying,' George went on. 'Most experienced pilots wouldn't have made a better forced landing than you did. You've got a brilliant flying future ahead of you.'

In spite of everything, Francesca felt a glow of warmth at George's remark. But then, all of a sudden, she imagined her next flight – later that week, next week, whenever it might be – and she felt a sense of panic. Something told her she wouldn't be able to do it. The longer she waited, the worse it would be. The thought of what Doug had done would stick in her mind like a seed and grow there, filling her head with fear. Afraid her hand would begin to tremble, she quickly put down her cup of coffee.

And then it came to her. If she were ever going to fly again, it had to be as soon as possible. She sat up and turned to George.

'George,' she began, 'would you consider allowing me to take the other Cessna for a flight?'

'Of course,' George replied. 'When?'

'Now,' Francesca answered.

'What!' George exclaimed.

'Now. This minute,' Francesca said firmly. 'I know that if I don't go today, I'll never get in the pilot's seat again; I'll completely lose my nerve.'

George shook his head immediately. 'No, Francesca, I'm sorry, but it's quite out of the question. You've just had a terrible experience; you're not thinking straight, you're far too emotional. Look at you, you're shaking.'

Francesca looked at George desperately. 'Just one short flight,' she said. 'Take off and land, like my first solo. If I don't, I'll never fly again.'

'Well, I'll come with you,' George said.

'No, it has to be solo,' Francesca insisted.

George closed his eyes, then opened them. He looked across at Tom. 'You tell her, Tom. You're her boyfriend. Perhaps you can make her see some sense.'

Francesca turned to Tom. He was looking down, his head in his hands. Now, he looked up. Francesca watched him. For a moment, he reminded her of Andrea with his head held high like that.

'I think you should let her go, George,' he said quietly. 'I think you should let her decide.'

George stared at Tom in shock. Then, after thinking for a while longer, he finally gave a tiny nod of his head.

* * *

Less than half an hour later, Francesca was approaching the runway for the second time that day, in the other Flying Start Cessna, G-ABJN. She felt perfectly calm. She stopped the plane before the runway, turned into the wind, and did the power checks. Then she called the control tower.

'Norwich Tower. Golf Juliet November is ready to line up runway zero nine.'

'Golf Juliet November, please wait.'

Francesca did as instructed, guessing that another aircraft must be coming in. As she waited, she thought about Tom, about what he'd just done. George must have been quite certain that Tom would say this flight was a crazy idea. But he hadn't. He'd taken Francesca's side. He'd put his confidence in her and given her her freedom. That was the kind of love she wanted. He was the sort of person she could love.

A small two-engined plane flew past in front of her. She watched it land, first one of the main wheels, then the other, finally, the nose wheel – a good crosswind landing. Then came her call on the radio.

'Golf Juliet November, line up runway zero nine.'

Francesca released the brakes and moved the plane forward, then swung round onto the piano keys and stopped.

Only then did nerves grip her stomach. Did she really want to do this? Perhaps it wasn't such a good idea after all.

In the distance the other plane had disappeared from the runway. She waited. Then came the call. 'Golf Juliet November. You are cleared for take-off.'

Sitting there alone in the plane, she was suddenly overcome with fear as the memory of the forced landing came back to her. She had nearly died! What was she thinking of, going up there again? Down here on the ground she was safe.

The seconds passed. She had to do something. She could head back to the hangar or go ahead and take off. She stared through the windscreen down the runway, the white dotted line stretching away into the unknown. 'Like the rest of my life,' she thought to herself all of a sudden. Where would she be in one year's time? Would she have passed her private pilot's exams and be studying for her commercial licence? Would she still be living in England? Would she still be with Tom? And what about in five years' time? She had her whole life ahead of her. The mystery of the future suddenly filled her with excitement.

Without delaying a second longer, she steadily pushed in the throttle. The little plane began running forward immediately, quickly picking up speed. This was it.

She pulled back on the control column and felt the plane slowly lift into flight.